A STUDENT'S GUIDE TO
AMERICAN POLITICAL THOUGHT

ISI GUIDES TO THE MAJOR DISCIPLINES

GENERAL EDITOR   EDITOR

JEFFREY O. NELSON   JEREMY BEER

PHILOSOPHY   *Ralph M. McInerny*

LITERATURE   *R. V. Young*

LIBERAL LEARNING   *James V. Schall, S.J.*

THE STUDY OF HISTORY   *John Lukacs*

THE CORE CURRICULUM   *Mark C. Henrie*

U.S. HISTORY   *Wilfred M. McClay*

ECONOMICS   *Paul Heyne*

POLITICAL PHILOSOPHY   *Harvey C. Mansfield*

PSYCHOLOGY   *Daniel N. Robinson*

CLASSICS   *Bruce S. Thornton*

A Student's Guide to American Political Thought

George W. Carey

ISI Books

Wilmington, Delaware

A Student's Guide to American Political Thought is made possible by grants from the Lee and Ramona Bass Foundation, the Huston Foundation, Barre Seid Foundation, and the Wilbur Foundation. The Intercollegiate Studies Institute gratefully acknowledges their support.

Cataloging-in-Publication Data

Carey, George W.
    A student's guide to American political thought / George W. Carey.
    —1st ed. — Wilmington, Del. : ISI Books, 2004.

    p; / cm.

    Includes bibliographic references.
    ISBN: 1- 932236-42-2 (pbk.)

    1. Political science—United States. 2. Political parties—United
        States. 3. Political science—philosophy. I. Title.

JA84.U6 C37 2004   2004104557
320/.0973—dc22   0410

ISI Books
Post Office Box 4431
Wilmington, DE 19807-0431

Cover and interior design by Sam Torode

CONTENTS

INTRODUCTION

WHAT IS AMERICAN POLITICAL THEORY? There is no universal agreement about what constitutes politics or the political, as the efforts to define the boundaries of political science over the decades will attest. Yet, at a minimum, "political theory" clearly is concerned with core questions relating to government and how authoritative decisions are made in a society. Among these questions are: On what principles is the government based? How is authority allocated within it? What are its primary purposes? Are their limitations to its powers? How can it be altered? And upon what assumptions regarding human nature does it seem to be based?

Viewed from this perspective, the American experience provides a rich source of theory in many particulars. Most of the early charters left the colonists free to use their own best ideas in establishing political order, the terms of which were spelled out in written documents. Moreover, during the long period of England's "benign neglect," which extended into the middle of the eighteenth century, the colonists grew accustomed to refining their processes and institutions of government. Thus, we have numerous documents relating directly to core concerns of governance that reveal a good deal about the American political thought of the pre-founding period. To these, of course, must be added those ordering documents of the founding era with which we are far more familiar: the state constitutions, the Articles of Confederation, and, most importantly, the Constitution itself. Indeed, after the adoption of the Constitution, American political thought concentrates to a great extent on issues arising from its interpretation.

It is frequently remarked that times of crisis or disorder produce political theory, if only because such times compel hard thinking about the failings of the old order and the goals of the new. This is certainly true with regard to American political theory. The movement toward separation from Great Britain that culminated with the Declaration of Independence provides us with insights into certain enduring principles of American political thought. Likewise, conditions during the "critical period" under the Articles of Confederation that led to the Philadelphia Convention also generated a good deal of political thinking about the requisites for effective government over an extensive territory. The records we have of the deliberations of the Constitutional Convention, the subsequent debates in the ratifying conventions, as well as the printed essays on both sides of the ratification question (particularly, *The Federalist*)[1] are all core materials for students of American political theory. So too are the major speeches, debates, and works concerning our basic commitments as a people and the nature of our constitutional system that preceded and followed the Civil War.

The scope of American political theory also embraces a myriad of other sources, the criterion for inclusion being a broad one, namely, to what extent they bear upon the central questions involved with governance. This would certainly include public addresses and private correspondence of presidents, major public officials, prominent citizens, and the like; public and official documents, particularly those that proclaim national ideals, goals, or commitments; debates and literature dealing with perennial problems or competing conceptions of constitutional principles; commentaries on the Constitution; pronouncements of the Supreme Court on matters of constitutional doctrine; disputes over the proper role of government; the deliberations of Congress on constitutional issues; and, inter alia, suggested reforms of the constitutional system. All this and more constitute the raw materials of the field of American political theory.

Surveying the materials that fit within its parameters reveals the extent to which American political theory is tied to history. The field is by no means the exclusive domain of political scientists, though historians usually approach the same subject matter differently. In any event, what is apparent in most cases is that the materials do not speak for themselves; to appreciate their significance fully often requires an understanding of their context. Some of the most important provisions and principles of the Constitution, to take an obvious example, cannot be fully understood without an understanding of the political situation under the Articles of Confederation. Nor can one fully comprehend the Mayflower Compact without knowing about the experiences of the Puritans and their theological roots. Indeed, such contextual knowledge is essential for a comprehensive understanding of the political theory embedded in all of the primary documents, that is, those that are regarded as central to American political thought.

4

A field so closely tied to history is, understandably, also closely tied to what is called the American political tradition. Put another way, most of the documents at the center of American political theory—and the values, concerns, and preferences they embody—emerge out of the experiences and circumstances of the American people at different times and places. As such, these documents are integral to the American political tradition; they constitute its essence. Consequently, American political theory is in many ways a study of the American political tradition; the two terms are often used interchangeably, and appropriately so. In an important sense, then, a good deal of American political theory is abstracted from the political activities and experiences of Americans.

The upshot of this is that a course in American political theory will probably differ substantially from most other courses offered in the more general field of political theory that deal, chronologically or otherwise, with major theoretical works. One reason for this difference—and perhaps even for the manner in which American theory is tied to our tradition—might well be the dearth of first-rate political treatises produced by Americans. Indeed, it is generally agreed that only one such work merits being called a classic, namely, *The Federalist.* Some have argued that John C. Calhoun's *Disquisition on Government* (1851) deserves this distinction as well. A fine course in American political theory could center almost entirely on these two works, but most courses, while not ignoring these works, will deal with a wider range of materials.

What has been said to this point raises important concerns that will be addressed at greater length later in this guide. For instance: Is there one continuous American political tradition? If so, what are the theoretical roots of that

---

The following are among those works that offer primary documents and materials showing the linkage between the Western tradition and the colonial experience in the development of American constitutionalism: *The Founders' Constitution,* ed. Philip B. Kurland and Ralph Lerner, 5 vols. (Chicago, 1987; paperback edition: Indianapolis, 2000); *The Roots of Liberty,* ed. Ellis Sandoz (Columbia, MO, 1993); *Colonial Origins of the American Constitution,* ed. Donald Lutz (Indianapolis, 1998); and *The American Republic: Primary Sources,* ed. Bruce Frohnen (Indianapolis, 2002). Among works that trace the varied contributions to the development of American constitutions are: James McClellan, *Liberty, Order, and Justice* (Indianapolis, 2000); Donald Lutz, *The Origins of American Constitutionalism* (Baton Rouge, 1988); Russell Kirk, *The Roots of American Order* (Washington, DC, 1991; repr.Wilmington, DE, 2003); Trevor Colbourn, *The Lamp of Experience* (Indianapolis, 1998); David H. Fischer, *Albion's Seed* (New York, 1989); and M. Stanton Evans, *The Theme Is Freedom* (Washington, DC 1994).

tradition? When did it begin? Or is there more than one political tradition? And, if so, what are the contours of these traditions?

COMMON GROUND: THE FOUNDING ERA

The field of American political theory, as we have indicated, embraces a massive body of primary materials that has swelled enormously in recent decades. This means that courses in American political theory will vary significantly in both substance and approach, depending largely on the predilections of the instructor. Furthermore, both the meaning of and relationships among the primary materials at the core of the American political tradition are legitimately subject to varying interpretations.

It would be wrong to conclude, however, that such courses will have no common ground in their substance or approach. A uniqueness attaches to the American political tradition that serves to provide a focus to its study. The source of this uniqueness derives from the query put by Alexander Hamilton at the beginning of the first essay in *The Federalist*, "whether societies of men are really capable or not, of establishing good government from reflection and choice, or whether they are forever destined to depend, for their political constitutions, on accident or force." This, he believed, was the overriding question facing the American people at the time of the ratification struggle— and not only the American people but all mankind as well. The affirmative answer given this question with the adoption of the Constitution has served to provide a fixed point of reference for students in the field.

That the Constitution should serve this function is quite understandable. It was not ordained or sanctioned by the gods, nor was it "given" to the people by a mythical lawgiver. Rather, it is a written document, the result of a deliberative process, that can be considered the embodiment of the "constitutive will" of a people; that is, the Constitution spells out in some detail the processes and institutions by which the people, acting in their constituent capacity, have consented to be governed. It is "fundamental law" in the sense that it is unalterable by the government it creates. Madison, writing in *Federalist* 53, conveys this understanding of the Constitution's status when he distinguishes "between a constitution established by the people, and unalterable by government" and systems such

8

as the English one, in which legislatures have "a full power to change the form of government."

In fact, at no subsequent period in their history have the American people ever seriously entertained the idea of undertaking a new act of founding; that is, of deliberating as a people with the end of producing a new constitution that would embody their "constitutive will." Quite the contrary. There is a common understanding (a "constitutional morality," if you will) that the Constitution should be amended only when there is a compelling need. Alarm is frequently expressed by politicians and opinion leaders at the mere prospect of constitutional conventions meeting at the request of state legislatures to draft specific amendments (e.g., amendments requiring a balanced budget, sanctioning voluntary prayers in public schools, or limiting terms of office) for fear that these conventions might go too far and thereby destroy the handiwork of the framers. In the popular culture, at least, it would appear that the motives and deeds of the framers are beyond reproach.

The Declaration of Independence and the Articles of Confederation are also central documents in the American political tradition. We know that without separation from Great Britain, the choice of which Hamilton writes would not have been possible. Although controversy surrounds the Declaration's precise role, import, and status within the tradition, its significance cannot be denied because, among other things, it justifies our separation from Great Britain, sets forth "self-evident" "truths," and advances the proposition that governments derive their "just powers from the consent of the governed." In addition, as Thomas Jefferson wrote nearly fifty years after the event, the Declaration "was intended to be an expression of the American mind," and "its authority rests . . . on the harmonizing sentiments of the day, whether expressed in conversation, in letters, printed essays, or in the elementary books of public right, as Aristotle, Cicero, Locke, Sidney, &c." Most students of the period agree with Jefferson's assessment.

In general, any course in American political theory—save, perhaps, those devoted to some special period or concern—will deal with the "founding era," as it is commonly dubbed. This era is defined in various ways, but most scholars would place its beginning shortly after the period of "benign neglect" that ended in the early 1760s when Britain began to reassert more stringent control over the colonies. There is less consensus in fixing its cut-off point, but most agree that it runs at least into the early years of the nineteenth century. During this entire period the American people were obliged by circumstances to think about fundamental political values and to make authoritative and strategic decisions that would bind subsequent generations. As a consequence, to use a metaphor, the founding period can be looked upon as both the center of and the energizing force behind the ever-expanding universe of American political theory.

The Founding: Search for Deeper Meaning

That the founding era should enjoy the special status it does is not surprising, since we still live under the forms of the Constitution. But the fact that it provides a common ground for students of American theory has not produced a consensus about either its character or about what the founders were really up to. With increasing frequency since the turn of the twentieth century, many scholars have raised troubling questions about the founders and their motives. Did they really believe in republican government, or were they intent on constructing a system that would protect elite interests under the rubric of a republican form? Can we take them at their word, believing what they said and wrote publicly, or were they advancing a hidden agenda?

At still another level questions have arisen over what values or theories dominated during this period and whether or not it is marked by a theoretical continuity. Taken as a whole, the disputes that have arisen over the character of our founding have led some to conclude that any clear understanding of the American political tradition and the values that have informed it is next to impossible. Put otherwise, there seems to be an inverse relationship between the scholarly attention devoted to this period and our understanding of it, as evidenced by the proliferation of interpretations that have given rise to these critical questions.

There are reasons for these disputes. To begin with, there are those who seek an understanding of the American political tradition, of which the founding era is taken to be the core, from both a broader and "deeper" perspective. They seek, that is, to incorporate American political thought into more systematic philosophical schools or enduring strains of thought within the Western tradition, thereby rendering it more coherent and "whole." In light of the fact that American political thought at its best is usually narrowly focused, these efforts are understandable. *The Federalist*, for example, is praised largely for its nuts-and-bolts approach, not for its metaphysical insights or theoretical coherence. Consequently, those concerned with the deeper questions concerning the origin and purposes of the state, the limits of law, the meaning of justice, and the like, find even the major works of the American tradition wanting. Their efforts are directed toward filling this void.

These endeavors would seem destined to produce different understandings of the tradition, if only because different individuals are bound to see different connections between American and Western political thought. Additionally, interpretations of major philosophers in the Western tradition often vary, sometimes significantly—John Locke comes readily to mind in this regard—so that views will differ over the nature and extent of their connection to the American tradition. Furthermore, any endeavor to demonstrate the influence of a particular philosopher or school of thought on the founders—beyond particular, limited concerns or issues—involves showing a direct cause-and-effect relationship that is extremely difficult to establish with a high degree of certainty.

Yet another major reason for the confusing and contradictory accounts of the beliefs and motivations of the founding fathers is the effect of political ideology—that is, the political perspectives of scholars that often channel their vision and color their analyses and interpretations. This is not at all surprising given the fact that partisan political advantage can be derived by linking one's desired programs and policy goals to the underlying values of the American tradition, particularly to the founders' ideals. Simply linking an ideology to a respected tradition lends legitimacy to the goals of that ideology, all the more so if a scenario can be constructed that shows how those goals, sanctioned by our forefathers, have been misunderstood, subverted, or ignored over the decades. Such endeavors usually involve tinkering somewhat with the raw materials of the tradition.

Contemporary controversies surrounding constitutional interpretation illustrate an important dimension of this process. Given the reverence most Americans have for their Constitution, no party in a constitutional dispute wants to be in the position of opposing the "intentions" of the founders. A key question thus becomes: What were their intentions with respect to the issue at hand? More often than not, this leads to the proliferation of conflicting positions that, in turn, are based on different and often incompatible views, frequently couched in theoretical terms, about what the framers intended. Or, when the intent of the framers seems clear but unacceptable to one of the contending parties, recourse can then be had to the tactic of asking: In light of changing circumstances and values, what would the framers think or do today?

Precisely because the founding period is so crucial for understanding the character of the American political tradition, students should be fully aware of the limitations of those approaches that strive to give it a deeper meaning, as well as the political factors (including ideology) that come into play in interpreting the founders' motives and beliefs. The two are not, we should emphasize, mutually exclusive.

Keeping all this in mind, a brief survey of the major accounts of the founders' motivations and goals, as well as these accounts' development and interrelationship, should serve to illustrate their limitations and why it is that controversy surrounds the founding.

DISINGENUOUS FOUNDERS?

While no one factor accounts for the unsettled state of American political theory, there can be no question about the impact of two works that appeared during the "Progressive Era" of the early twentieth century: James Allen Smith's *The Spirit of American Government* (New York, 1907) and Charles A. Beard's *An Economic Interpretation of the Constitution of the United States* (New York, 1913). Smith's work set forth a theme that is now commonplace in American government and American history texts, namely, that the Constitution was designed to curb the democratic impulses unleashed by the Revolution. Smith noted that of the fifty-five delegates to the Philadelphia Convention—most of them from the well-to-do and more conservative segments of society—only six had signed the Declaration of Independence. He contended that their contributions to the deliberations clearly show that they had no love for popular government and sought to curb, through an elaborate system of checks and balances, what they considered to be its probable excesses. Primarily for this reason, Smith argued, they sought a stronger central government that would be resistant to change and public opinion. He maintained further that the founders' "real" motives, as opposed to those garnered from their public statements, could best be determined by attending to what they said behind the Convention's closed doors. Thus did he bring into question the motives of the framers, casting doubt on their goals as well as their democratic credentials.

Two further aspects of Smith's assault are noteworthy. First, he suggested that the theory of the founding period was bifurcated; that on one side were the true democrats, such as Thomas Jefferson, Thomas Paine, and Samuel Adams, and on the other those, such as the Philadelphia Convention delegates, who distrusted the people. This hypothesis of theoretical bifurcation reappears frequently, in one form or another, in other accounts of the founding period, the major variant stressing instead the differences between Hamilton and Jefferson. And second, Smith partitioned the founding period along still another dimension by arguing that the democratic forces, which predominated at the time of the Declaration, had lost out to the forces of "reaction" by the time of the Philadelphia Convention. This theme also frequently reappears in other versions of the theoretical landscape and dynamics of this period. Its major variations surround what accounts for this change—whether, for instance, there really had been a sea change in popular feeling or whether the reactionary nature of the Constitution resulted from the maneuvering of the elites who dominated the Convention.

Beard's book has had a far deeper and more lasting effect on the scholarship of the founding era, particularly with regard to the question of the motives of those who drafted the Constitution. Beard focused on *Federalist* 10, an essay in which Madison wrote of the "rights of property," held the role of government to be the regulation of various "interests"—"landed," "manufacturing," "mercantile," and "moneyed"—and declared that "those who hold and those who are without property have ever formed distinct interests in society." Beard claimed to have found in this essay a "theory of economic determinism." After surveying the general economic and political landscape of the time immediately prior to the Convention and the economic interests of the delegates, Beard concluded that the Constitution was the direct result of the efforts of a small, elite group whose members were attached to one of four "personality interests": "money, public securities, manufactures, and trade and shipping." He also argued that the institutions of government were carefully designed to advance these interests, while protecting the "private rights of property" from leveling majorities.

The impact of Beard's work has been enormous. While many of his findings and conclusions have been thoroughly refuted, he can be regarded as the father of a subdiscipline in history and political science that emphasizes the role of economic interests in accounting for the twists and turns in the American political tradition. Equally if not more important, his reliance on *Federalist* 10 as the point of departure for his study has served to channel the attention of students to this particular essay. Even many of those who are skeptical of his analysis of Madison's position have come to accept Beard's conclusion that the underlying theory of the Constitution is set forth in *Federalist* 10. Indeed, the arguments presented in that essay have been subjected to countless analyses over the decades in an effort to gain a deeper insight into the theoretical foundations of our political order or to discern more clearly the operating assumptions of the founders. Consequently, thanks mainly to Charles Beard, *Federalist* 10 is examined with some care in virtually every course in American political theory. And, not surprisingly, since the appearance of *An Economic Interpretation* James Madison's status as a political theorist has surged. Many scholars, going beyond *Federalist* 10 to examine all of his writings, have come to regard him as the principal theorist of the Constitution.

The legacy of the Smith/Beard approach to understanding the founding period and, in particular, the motives of those who drafted the Constitution is reflected in another enormously influential work, Robert Dahl's *Preface to Democratic Theory* (Chicago, 1956). In this work, Dahl breaks Madison's thought down into a number of propositions that he then subjects to careful scrutiny from a positivist perspective. In his view, the founders substantially accepted what he terms the "Madisonian ideology." This ideology, which rationalized the processes and institutions of the Constitution, was designed to protect select minorities of wealth and status from the ravages of popular majorities. Dahl's work, like Beard's, generated a strong adverse reaction in many quarters, much of it prompted by Dahl's contention that key terms and concepts in Madison's theory, such as "tyranny" and "rights," were meaningless.

For devastating rejoinders to the Beardian thesis see: Forrest McDonald, *We the People* (Chicago, 1958); and Robert E. Brown, *Charles Beard and the Constitution* (Princeton, NJ, 1956). A critique of the progressive account of the founding is George W. Carey, *In Defense of the Constitution* (Indianapolis, 1995). On Madison, *Federalist* 10, and Charles Beard see: Douglass Adair, *Fame and the Founding Fathers*, ed. Trevor Colbourn (Indianapolis, 1998); Ronald Peters Jr. provides a trenchant critical analysis of Dahl's argument in "Political Theory, Political Science, and *The Preface*," *Political Science Reviewer* 7 (1977).

Its major impact was to bolster the view that Madison was to a considerable degree the "philosopher" of the Constitution—a view which, though widely held, is largely untenable.

It should be remarked that the Smith/Beard approach, beyond holding that the foundations of our constitutional tradition are basically undemocratic, would have us believe that we cannot take at face value what many key individuals of the founding generation said. For his part, Dahl accepts the characterization of the founders as an undemocratic elite, but he also holds that the ideology which sought to rationalize their position in democratic terms does not make sense. In his account, as in Smith and Beard's, the democratic or republican strains of our political tradition were subverted because of the self-serving motives of a powerful elite.

A BROADER PICTURE

Dahl's treatment of the founders was narrow and limited, based on the unarticulated assumption that an examination of Madison's writings, principally those in *The Federalist*, is sufficient for understanding the concerns and motivations of the framers. But despite this shortcoming, his findings and conclusions—along with those of Smith and Beard—are reflected in broader theoretical analyses of the founding era. One such analysis is Vernon L. Parrington's highly regarded two-volume *Main Currents in American Thought* (New York, 1927). This work, dedicated to James Allen Smith, endeavored to place key elements of the founders' thought into the wider context of Western political thought. Parrington emphasized what he understood to be the derivative character of American political thought; specifically, he viewed the major competing schools of thought at the time of our founding as having roots in the broader Western tradition. For example, in his account, the philosophy of "English Liberalism," an amalgam of ideas taken from the theories of James Harrington, John Locke, and Adam Smith, prevailed by default in the period leading up to the Constitution. This liberalism, according to Parrington, embraced capitalism, stressed individualism and the inviolability of property rights, and justified the pursuit of economic interest free from restraints and control by government. Later, because of the circumstances peculiar to the new nation, liberal theory assumed a distinctly American character; the most important deviation from its English counterpart being the felt need for a strong centralized government to advance dominant economic interests.

Parrington also emphasized the importance of the emergence of a French Romantic philosophy deeply indebted to Rousseau and the ideals of the French Revolution. While elements of this philosophy were present prior to the Constitutional Convention, Parrington believed its main impact was felt once the new government was set in motion and that it reached fruition with Jefferson's election to the presidency. Parrington took pains to illustrate that French Romantic thought differed from English Liberalism on most fundamental issues, the most basic being that the former was idealistic, egalitarian, and concerned with the realization of the common good, whereas the latter concentrated on the promotion of capitalism. Parrington saw the differences between these two philosophies reflected in the writings and actions of Hamilton and Jefferson, particularly in their differences over the effects of centralization. As Parrington would have it, Hamilton was antagonistic toward agrarianism, with its orientation towards local control, whereas Jefferson viewed this localism as the essence of popular government. This difference points to one of the perennial and most fundamental issues in American political theory, local versus national control, usually discussed or debated under the rubric of "federalism," which we will discuss in more detail below.

While Smith and Parrington were critical of the framers because their Constitution centralized political power, thereby undermining the agrarian democracy central to Jefferson's vision, Herbert Croly—who can justifiably be called the father of modern progressivism—comes to almost the opposite conclusion in his major work, *The Promise of American Life* (New York, 1909). In this work, published shortly after Smith's, Croly stressed that the decentralization of political authority, an outgrowth of Jeffersonian thinking, presents the major obstacle to the fulfillment of the "national promise." Picturing the founding period largely in terms of a contest between the visions of Hamilton and Jefferson, Croly praised Hamilton, not for his ends, but for his awareness of what was necessary for their realization, namely, a more powerful central government. On the other hand, he held that Jefferson's vision—his goals and values—corresponded far more closely than Hamilton's to the "promise" of American life. Only the issue of centralization and its relation to democracy—albeit a most critical one—serves to separate Croly from

Parrington in any meaningful way.

Croly and Parrington merit attention because in their hands the American political tradition bears all the characteristics of a morality play, an ongoing competition between the forces of good and evil. For both men, the conflicting visions of Hamilton and Jefferson (along with their subsequent permutations) suffuse and explain much of America's political past. Their account also manages to situate the more specific "findings" of Smith and Beard into a more comprehensive and coherent whole, Parrington even supplying the "deeper" philosophical understanding of the American political tradition by relating it to the broader currents in Western political thought. Along with Dahl, Smith, and Beard, Croly and Parrington seem certain about what theories, visions, or goals constitute the good. They simply differ about the best way of achieving that good.

Given these similarities, we can ask: To what extent are these theories skewed by an ideology? Do they reflect the failure of the American system to move rapidly enough, if at all, in the direction of the good that they envision? Do their proponents, in other words, share roughly the same political agenda? These are the questions that those students embarking on studies of American political theory should constantly bear in mind when evaluating accounts of our founding, particularly the more comprehensive ones that claim to have discovered the dynamics of our political tradition.

TOWARD A SYNTHESIS:
AN EVEN BROADER PICTURE

The Liberal Tradition in America (New York, 1955), written by Harvard professor Louis Hartz, advanced and defended the thesis that the American political tradition, particularly from the time of the Declaration of Independence, could be explained in terms of John Locke's liberalism or variants thereof. Locke's political thinking, he believed, fit the conditions and circumstances of America hand in glove, especially because America lacked a feudal tradition. The Mayflower Compact, for instance, was akin to Locke's social contract, and the frontier resembled his state of nature. A rugged individualism, the growth of capitalism, the Horatio Alger myth, the sanctity of private property, the rejection of socialism, the concern about majority oppression and minority rights, and other fundamental American beliefs and values could be accounted for by reference to Locke. So strong was Locke's hold on our tradition that

Hartz worried about the conformity of thought manifest in the unwillingness of the American people to tolerate alternative paradigms.

The understanding of Croly, Parrington, and other Progressives concerning the overriding goals of the founders fit very well into Hartz's interpretation. Hartz agreed with them that most of the founders were suspicious of the people. Yet his reading differed from theirs on at least one fundamental point, in that he contended that the goals of the elite were widely shared among the people. From Hartz's vantage point, the founders' mistrust of the people was ill-founded, as evidenced by the eventual emergence of a "democratic capitalism" that would have warmed Hamilton's heart. Hartz provides, in the last analysis, what can be termed a single-theory explanation of the American political tradition, a tradition that embraces as its "civil theology" the principal tenets of Lockean liberalism—rationalism, secularism, and individualism.

Hartz's work is still generally considered to be the locus classicus for the articulation of the liberal interpretation of the American political tradition. But he is far from being alone. Many others have also stressed the Lockean foundations of both the Declaration of Independence and the Constitution, although in terms somewhat different than those of Hartz. Some have held that Locke's teachings fit into the "modern" school of Western political thought in which the ends of political association have been lowered from those upheld by classical thinkers—that is, lowered from the virtues and cultivation of the common good that the ancients taught as the proper ends of politics "down" to providing for individual liberty, rights, and gratification. Others have seen Locke as providing the basic principles of our constitutional order—for example, the separation of powers, the consent of the governed, and the rule of law—which should not be seen as antagonistic, but rather as fully receptive, to the classical virtues. Still others regard Locke's philosophy as a commonsense embodiment of the better elements of Western political thought.

Since the 1960s, the liberal or Lockean paradigm of the American founding has been challenged with increasing intensity by those who have advanced an alternative "republican" paradigm. While this paradigm is also far from being monolithic, one version even locating the roots of this republicanism in ancient Greece, it clearly differs from the liberal interpretation in holding that the political thought of the founding era was dominated by a concern with the common good and the belief that individuals should subordinate their self-interest to the good of the community. Also central to this republicanism is the belief that government and society bear the responsibility to preserve and promote civic virtue, a principle that rests on the belief that the health and very existence of the republic depend on the moral fiber of its citizenry. In sum, in the liberal and republican paradigms we find two essentially different views of the values and goals that motivated the founding generation: the public-spiritedness of republicanism and the individualism and acquisitiveness of liberalism.

Clearly, the substance of the republican paradigm bears more than a cousinly resemblance to the principal elements of Parrington's French Romantic school of thought and to the non-acquisitive, cooperative individuals in Croly's vision of the national promise. It conforms in important particulars, this is to say, with the Progressive school. One of the principal works that advances this republican interpretation, Gordon Wood's *Creation of the American Republic* (Chapel Hill, NC, 1969), even incorporates the view, first advanced by James Allen Smith, that republicanism prevailed at the time of the Declara-

29

tion only to lose out to liberalism later in the founding era.

While it seems clear that both the modern liberal and republican paradigms are rooted in accounts of our political tradition and, in particular, on perceptions of the founding period that emerged much earlier in the twentieth century, they highlight a critical question that the earlier accounts did not. The liberal paradigm suggests that our system rests on the accommodation of competing interests, whereas from the republican perspective it ultimately seeks to promote the virtue of its citizenry. Thus, for students of American political theory, the question becomes: Is the American system anchored in virtue or interest?

The following reflect both differences within and between different schools of thought concerning the major theoretical influences on the founding generation: J. G. A. Pocock, *The Machiavellian Moment* (Princeton, NJ, 1975); Bernard Bailyn, *The Ideological Origins of the American Revolution* (Cambridge, MA, 1967); Gordon Wood, *The Creation of the American Republic* (Chapel Hill, NC, 1969); Thomas Pangle, *The Spirit of Modern Republicanism* (Chicago, 1988); John Diggins, *The Lost Soul of American Politics* (New York, 1984); Caroline Robbins, *The Eighteenth-Century Commonwealthman* (Cambridge, MA, 1959); and Joyce Appleby, *Liberalism and Republicanism in the Historical Imagination* (Cambridge, MA, 1992).

SERIOUS COMPLICATIONS

Alexis de Tocqueville, generally regarded as the most insightful and provocative observer of the American people and their culture, began the first of his two-volume work, *Democracy in America,*[2] by commenting on the necessity of exploring the roots of American society in order to understand the direction of its growth. He emphasized the New England experience, pointing to the importance of the colonists' political institutions and practices and the impact of Christian beliefs. Tocqueville's observations and approach highlight perhaps the most telling objection to virtually all the interpretive schools of thought we have discussed thus far, namely, their tendency to treat the founding era as distinct and largely isolated from the American experience that preceded it.

It comes as no surprise, therefore, that some scholars do look upon the founding period in light of the broader American political experience that dates back to the earliest settlements. Some see an organic development of American political institutions and practices that smoothed the transition to political independence and provided the basic framework for the Constitution. Others emphasize the influence of Christian thought, especially that of Reformed

Protestantism, on the outlook and lives of the colonists, an influence that continued, perhaps with less intensity, into the founding period. The consideration of Christianity and the experiences of the colonies, particularly those with Puritan foundations, complicates the picture of the founding in significant ways. First, it suggests that liberalism was by no means as pervasive as its proponents claim; that, indeed, even if the values and goals of liberalism were prevalent during the founding, they are perhaps best viewed as operating within a wider cultural framework informed primarily by Protestant values and virtues. Second, to the extent that Protestant Christianity provided individuals' moral bearings, the role of civic virtues, central to the republican account, is brought into question. In other words, for an adequate comprehension of the moral dimensions of the period, it may well be that the Bible and Christian teaching and practices are more important than the more worldly civic virtues central to republicanism. Finally, as Barry Shain points out in *The Myth of American Individualism* (Princeton, NJ, 1994), the communal way of life practiced by Christians contradicts the proposition, embraced in different ways and to different degrees by both liberalism and republicanism, that individualism is central to the

American political tradition. Rather, the way of life of early Americans was centered in particular localities, whose residents were resistant or antagonistic to direction from a distant, central authority.

The place of Christianity in the American tradition raises questions that simmer even today. It is well known that religion was central to the life of the early New England settlers. John Winthrop even envisioned "a city on a hill" that would be a Christian commonwealth marked by an extremely close and harmonious relationship been civil and religious authorities. Over the decades, this dream faded, in part because the new settlers lacked the religious intensity of their earlier counterparts. It is not insignificant that the first words of the Pilgrims' Mayflower Compact (1620) are "In the name of God, Amen," while those of the Constitution are "We the People." Furthermore, as the colonies developed, the ties between civil and religious authorities loosened, in part to promote peace and harmony among the growing multiplicity of Protestant denominations, some of the more prominent of which actually sought independence from civil government. The position of these denominations is articulated in part during the founding period in James Madison's *Memorial and Re-*

monstrance, published anonymously in 1785, which opposed assessments by the state for religious purposes.

Yet there is overwhelming evidence that many in the founding generation believed that religion was necessary to preserve and promote the virtue necessary for good government—and particularly for decent and orderly republican government. Article 3 of the Northwest Ordinance reads: "Religion, morality and knowledge being necessary to good government and the happiness of mankind, schools and the means of education shall forever be encouraged." Countless similar citations could be adduced to this same effect, but George Washington's Farewell Address stands as the most emphatic and authoritative: "Of all the dispositions and habits which lead to political prosperity, Religion and morality are indispensable supports. . . . Whatever may be conceded to the influence of refined education on minds of peculiar structure, reason and experience both forbid us to expect that National morality can prevail in exclusion of religious principle." Significantly, almost four decades later, Tocqueville observed that Americans of all persuasions and "ranks" believed that religion "was indispensable to the maintenance of republican institutions."

Nor, in this connection, can the influence of Christian

teachings on the founders be ignored, particularly in their efforts to construct an enduring republican government. To begin with, we may assume that their Christian understanding of the order of being, with humans situated somewhere between God and beast, precluded them from seeking to restructure society with the end of bringing heaven to earth. So, too, their understanding of the fallen state of man certainly played some role in their thinking about the Constitution and the safeguards it should provide.

Certainly, from simply a pragmatic standpoint, many framers saw a compelling need for religion. For this reason and others, many scholars find it difficult to believe that they subscribed to anything resembling the "wall-of-separation doctrine" enshrined by the Supreme Court in the middle of the twentieth century. From the founders'

The following deal with the messages, influences, and role of religion during the founding era: *The Political Sermons of the American Founding*, ed. Ellis Sandoz (Indianapolis, 1991); Ellis Sandoz, *A Government of Laws* (Columbia, MO, 2001); James H. Hutson, *Religion and the Founding of the American Republic* (Washington, DC, 1998); Mark Noll, *Christians in the American Revolution* (Grand Rapids, MI, 1977); Alan Heimert, *Religion and the American Mind: From the Great Awakening to the Revolution* (Cambridge, MA, 1966); Nathan O. Hatch, *The Sacred Cause of Liberty* (New Haven, CT, 1977); and Daniel Dreisbach, *Thomas Jefferson and the Wall of Separation between Church and State* (New York, 2002).

point of view, the First Amendment was not designed to erect such a wall, but rather to prevent the establishment of a national religion and to leave matters concerning church-state relations in the hands of the state governments. The present understanding of the relationship between government and religion suggests that, over the decades, secularism, sometimes in the form of outright hostility toward religion, has flourished to the extent that the founders' understanding of the important relationship between religion and politics is frequently minimized or ignored. In any event, this aspect of the American political tradition remains highly controversial and promises to remain so for the indefinite future.

MULTIPLE INFLUENCES

Single-theory interpretations of the founding era, along with those that picture it in terms of a battle between the forces of good and evil, are now often viewed as presenting only a partial, and sometimes distorted, account. There is increasing awareness that multiple influences and motivations were operating within the founding generation. This awareness produces an even more confusing account of the era, but one that is also probably more faithful to reality.

The colonists clearly sought to preserve the better portions of their English heritage. They had long enjoyed the common law rights and protections that had emerged from the English tradition. To take but one example, Article 39 of the Magna Carta (1215), the foundational document of English liberties, provides: "No freeman shall be taken or imprisoned, or disseised, or outlawed, or banished, or any ways destroyed, nor will we pass upon him, nor will we send upon him, unless by the lawful judgment of his peers, or by the law of the land." Five centuries later, we find that among the rights listed in the Massachusetts Constitution of 1780, widely regarded as the Rolls-Royce of the state constitutions adopted after the Declaration of Independence, is the guarantee that "no subject shall be arrested, imprisoned, despoiled . . . or deprived of his life, liberty, or estate; but by the judgment of his peers, or the law of the land." Beginning in the middle of the seventeenth century, the phrase "due process" gradually came to replace the expression "law of the land," so that we may say that the origins of the "due process" clauses of the Fifth Amendment and the Fourteenth Amendment to the Constitution, among other liberties we enjoy, are found in the Magna Carta.

The Revolutionary War, many scholars contend, was a "reactionary" revolution in the sense that the colonists were fighting for a restoration of the English liberties that they had once enjoyed during the "benign neglect" period. Edmund Burke, the great English statesman of the founding era who sought reconciliation with the colonies, argued that the colonists' discontent stemmed from the deprivation of liberties to which they had grown accustomed. Certainly their claim of "no taxation without representation" and their protests against illegal searches and seizures and the housing and quartering of troops possessed great weight because they were based on the common law. In fact, many of the grievances against King George III that constitute the bulk of the Declaration of Independence concern Britain's violations of the common law.

The influence of classical and modern political thought on the founders is also evident. While, as we have suggested above, it is difficult in many cases to show a direct connection between the thought and actions of the founders and a given political thinker or school of thought, there are cases where this connection seems clear. That John Locke had an impact is beyond question, particularly with regard to the opening paragraphs of the Declaration of

Independence, which spell out certain self-evident truths. William Blackstone's *Commentaries on the Laws of England* (1765–69) in providing a comprehensive understanding of the common law largely within the framework of Lockean thought, had a significant impact as well, particularly among lawyers. Major figures of the Scottish Enlightenment were also influential, especially David Hume, whose speculations on the possibility of an extended republic and whose analysis of factions greatly influenced James Madison. *Federalist* 10, the most widely read of *The Federalist* essays in modern times, borrows heavily from Hume's writings. That the views of Thomas Reid, a Scottish philosopher of the "common sense" school, carried great weight with James Wilson, a key player in the Philadelphia Convention and later a Supreme Court justice, can be readily seen in Wilson's *Lectures on the Law* (1790–91).

Montesquieu, the French political philosopher and author of *The Spirit of the Laws* (1748) deserves special mention because his views were widely quoted by the contending parties in the ratification struggle, the Anti-Federalists and the Federalists. The Anti-Federalists cited Montesquieu to the effect that a republic must be confined to a small territory with a small population having very similar inter-

While there is no question that the founders were influenced by history, the experience of other nations (both ancient and modern), and the major political writings of the Western tradition, there are two important facts to bear in mind relative to these influences. First, each nation has, so to speak, a unique cultural and political DNA. Thus, those teachings of the broader Western tradition that were assimilated into the American tradition were modified in important particulars to fit American circumstances and values. For instance, while Montesquieu is important for understanding the justification for our separation of powers, the separation we find in the Constitution differs fundamentally from that which he proposed. Montesquieu favored a "mixed" regime that would require an accommodation of the interests of the crown, aristocracy, and commons, a regime resembling that of the Great Britain of his time. The conditions of and prevailing thought in America, however, precluded any such arrangement. Simply put, America had no aristocracy or royalty, a fact noted at an early stage in the deliberations at Philadelphia. Consequently, the separation of powers found in the Constitution is one adapted to republican principles.

Second, though they were no doubt influenced by what
is generally regarded as modern Enlightenment thought—
e.g., Locke and the thinkers of the Scottish Enlightenment—the founders seem to have been unaffected by the

---

An overview of the intellectual currents and ideas that seemed to play
an important role in the outlook of the founding generation is
provided by Forrest McDonald, *Novus Ordo Seclorum: The Intellectual Origins of the Constitution* (Lawrence, KS, 1985); and Bernard
Bailyn, *Ideological Origins of the American Revolution* (Cambridge,
MA, 1967). A collection of the best essays of this period is *American
Political Writing during the Founding Era, 1760–1805*, ed. Charles S.
Hyneman and Donald Lutz, 2 vols. (Indianapolis, 1983). Among
collections of essays that approach the founding from a variety of
positions are: *Vital Remnants: America's Founding and the Western
Tradition*, ed. Gary L. Gregg II (Wilmington, DE, 1999) and *The
American Founding: Essays on the Formation of the Constitution*, ed.
J. Jackson Barlow, Leonard W. Levy, and Ken Masugi (New York,
1988). Two works dealing with the classical influences on American
thought are: Carl J. Richard, *The Founders and the Classics: Greece,
Rome, and the American Enlightenment* (Cambridge, MA, 1996) and
Meyer Reinhold, *Classica Americana: The Greek and Roman Heritage
in the United States* (Detroit, 1984). For interesting comparisons of
the French and Russian revolutions with the American see: Friedrich
von Gentz, *Origin and Principles of the American Revolution Compared
with the Origins and Principles of the French Revolution* and Stefan T.
Possony, *Reflections on the Russian Revolution* in *Three Revolutions*
(Westport, CT, 1976). For the founders' use of European political
theorists see: Donald Lutz, "The Relative Influence of European
Writers on Late-Eighteenth-Century American Political Thought,"
American Political Science Review 78 (1984).

more radical Enlightenment thinking that fueled the French Revolution. The American Revolution was of an almost entirely different order, lacking the ideological character of the French, which sought a radical reordering of society. Only snippets of the more radical French thought are to be found in the founders' writings, and these primarily in the writings and correspondence of Benjamin Franklin and Thomas Jefferson.

THE CONSTITUTION AND *THE FEDERALIST*

The deliberations of the Constitutional Convention are an invaluable source for understanding why the Constitution took the form it did. A year-long course could easily be constructed to explore the sources of conflict that were manifest, the politics of the delegations, the values that were brought to bear and their relationship to broader theories of governance, the various assumptions upon which the positions of the delegates were founded, and the areas of their tacit agreement. We know that the issue of equality of state representation in the Senate—a matter closely related to broader concerns about the balance between state and national authority—was the most critical, with the Convention nearly breaking apart over the Connecticut compromise. The problem of how to elect a president, which the delegates "solved" with the provision for an electoral college, reflected a concern over the separation of powers, i.e., how to provide for the electoral eligibility of a sitting president for subsequent terms without rendering him subservient to Congress. We see that to bring about a stronger union necessitated compromise on the issues of ending the slave trade and how slaves should be counted for purposes of representation. Though the delegates discussed the issue of voting qualifications—a discussion that revealed a range of attitudes towards popular control of government—they managed to duck the issue by passing it on to the states. And, significantly, there seemed to be a tacit agreement among the delegates that a far stronger national government than that provided by the Articles of Confederation was necessary. Even the so-called small-state or New Jersey Plan, offered by William Paterson as an alternative to the "nationalist" Virginia Plan, provided the national government with far greater authority than it possessed under the Articles. On these and other issues the deliberations of the Convention provide a rich source of materials for students of American political thought.

The Federalist is commonly regarded as the work that

best reveals the basic underlying theory of the Constitution, as well as the intentions of its drafters. In numerous Supreme Court cases, at least, it has been so regarded. But there is some dispute about the status of *The Federalist*. Some scholars regard it as mere "propaganda" that employs clever and selective arguments designed to garner support for ratification. Most scholars, however, view it as providing a deeper understanding of significant theoretical dimensions of the Constitution than that provided by the Convention deliberations or the debates in the state ratifying conventions. Few would deny, for instance, that *The Federalist* provides a framework for identifying and analyzing the major principles embodied in the Constitution. As such it has been and will continue to be a point of departure for critical studies of the constitutional framework and a benchmark against which to measure the degree of change in the constitutional system over time. For these reasons, virtually every course in American political theory, as well as many courses on American government, spends substantial time on certain of its essays.

The Federalist can be profitably viewed as a pathology of republicanism. This is to say that "Publius" wanted to show how the proposed system would avoid the calamities that had overtaken republics of the past. Of particular importance in this regard are four major elements at the core of his solution: (1) the creation of an extended republic with a multiplicity and diversity of interests; (2) the separation of powers; (3) the division of powers between state and national governments (commonly called "federalism" today); and (4) the institution of a constitutionalism that would operate to prevent the government from changing or abrogating through ordinary legislative processes the terms of the fundamental law embodied in the Constitution.

Federalist 10, to which we have already alluded, endeavors to show why the conditions associated with the extended republic—representation, and a multiplicity and diversity of interests—would serve to solve the disease "most incident to republican government," namely, majority factions. This essay should be read in conjunction with *Federalist* 9, in which it is contended that the new and improved principles of political science, most of them related to the separation of powers, allow for a stable republican government with ordered liberty. The latter third of essay 51 is also worthy of study because, in recapitulating the major argument of essay 10, it places in clear focus the anticipated dynamics of the extended republic that would prevent majority factions from ruling.

Beginning with essay 47 through most of essay 51, Madison deals with questions surrounding the separation of powers as a basic structural principle embedded in the Constitution. At the outset, he is clear that the separation of powers is needed because "tyranny" can be defined as the concentration of the legislative, executive, and judicial powers in the hands of one, the few, or the many. It is interesting to note that for Madison the *concentration* of powers itself constitutes tyranny, not the ends for which those powers are used. Tyranny exists wherever the potential for arbitrary and capricious government exists. The concentration of powers would allow legislators to pass laws favoring themselves and their families, friends, and political allies and to selectively administer and apply the laws through their control of the executive and judicial branches. Put another way, without an effective separation of powers, the rule of law, the very foundation of ordered liberty, would be in constant jeopardy. Thus, Madison's main concern is to maintain the separation between the different branches of government provided for in the Constitution.

Essays 48, 49, and 50 embody central elements of

Madison's political thought. In these essays he argues that "parchment barriers" will not suffice to keep the branches within their proper confines. On this score, Madison is most concerned with legislative encroachments, maintaining that "it is against the enterprising ambition of this department, that the people ought to indulge all their jealousy, and exhaust all their precautions." Nor does he believe it is prudent to use conventions elected by the people, either periodically or on specific occasions, to resolve differences between the branches. More likely than not—given the prestige, number, and influence of the legislators—those favorable to the legislative side, he believes, would dominate these conventions. But even if this were not the case, he fears, the resulting decisions would be dictated by passion, not reason. These considerations set the groundwork for his solution, presented in essay 51, for maintaining the constitutional separation of powers, a solution that involves weakening the predominant legislative branch by dividing it in two, and strengthening the executive branch by giving the president a qualified veto power. In the last analysis, however, Madison's solution rests on the connection between the interests of officeholders and "the constitutional rights" attached to their offices, a connection that assures that one governmental branch will use the constitutional means at its disposal to repel the encroachments of another. He openly confesses that this solution rests on "supplying, by opposite and rival interests, the defect of better motives."

The division of powers between the state and national governments, or federalism, is by far the most complicated topic in *The Federalist. Federalist* 39, an essay that delves into the national (unitary) and federal (confederate) characteristics of the Constitution, is a profitable point of departure for understanding these complications. As far as the distribution of powers is concerned, Madison considers the Constitution as providing for something in between a national, consolidated, or unitary system, wherein the central government would possess complete sovereignty, and a confederate system, wherein the component units would retain complete sovereignty. Hamilton subscribes to this understanding in *Federalist* 9, where he writes that under the proposed system the states will retain "certain exclusive, and very important, portions of the sovereign power." But there is some confusion about who or what is to arbitrate when there is conflict between the state and national governments over the extent of their respective powers. At one point (essay 39), Madison refers to a "tribunal," presumably the Supreme Court, and at another (essay 46) to "common constituents," presumably the people operating through Congress. Both Hamilton and Madison are concerned about the states encroaching on the national government, though they are ambivalent about which government ought to prevail in contests between the two. Madison's observation in *Federalist* 46 would seem to be in harmony with Hamilton's view (as presented in essay 27) that the people will have a propensity to favor the states over the national government, but that this propensity can be overcome by the national government through "manifest and irresistible proofs of better administration."

Finally, a theory of constitutionalism that regarded the Constitution as fundamental law, immune from change through normal political processes, obviously required some means for ensuring that the different governmental departments would not act contrary to its terms. The clearest and most extensive discussion of this understanding of the Constitution is found in *Federalist* 78, in which Hamilton sets forth and defends the doctrine of judicial review. Holding that it is within the special province of the Court to interpret the law, he reasons that when the Court finds an "irreconcilable variance" between a law passed by Congress and the Constitution, it is obliged to uphold the Constitution or "fundamental law." The Constitution is seen as embodying the *constitutive* will of the people—that is, the will that finds expression through the institutions created by the Constitution—which is more basic than and superior to their *political* will.

Hamilton regarded the Court as by far the weakest of the three branches, depending in the last analysis on the executive for the implementation of its decisions. Nor does he seem to have believed that the Court's power to declare acts of Congress unconstitutional would be frequently exercised. He sets forth what can be termed a "constitutional morality," namely, that the Court should exercise "judgment," not "will," the exercise of which was the province of the legislature. Nor does he argue that the Court should invalidate factious laws, but rather only those that clearly violate provisions of the Constitution. Hamilton's arguments seem to be directed against the Anti-Federalists, principally "Brutus," who contended that the Court's power of judicial review rendered it the most powerful branch, free to interpret the Constitution not by reference to its written provisions, but according to its "spirit."

In one fashion or another all these elements—the extended republic, the separation of powers, federalism, and
constitutionalism—have been subjects of controversy and
concern since Washington's inauguration, forming the
subject matter of a good deal of American political
thought. This is hardly surprising, since these elements
embodied political views that were novel or nearly so.
The extended republic theory completely turns on its head
traditional wisdom concerning the conditions necessary
for a republican government. In fact, according to the

Among the collections that provide primary materials highly relevant
to the Constitutional Convention and ratification struggle are: *The
Records of the Federal Convention of 1787*, ed. Max Farrand, 4 vols.
(1911; rev. ed., New Haven, CT, 1937) and *Supplement to Max
Farrand's "Records of the Federal Convention of 1787,"* ed. James H.
Hutson (New Haven, CT, 1987); *The Debates in the Several State
Conventions, on the Adoption of the Federal Constitution*, ed. Jonathan
Elliot, 5 vols. (1836; repr. New York, 1974) and *The Documentary
History of the Ratification of the Constitution*, ed. Merrill Jensen,
multiple vols. (Madison, WI, 1976–); and *Documents Illustrative of
the Formation of the Union of the American States*, ed. Charles C.
Tansill (Washington, DC, 1927). Notes taken at the convention,
primarily Madison's which are by far the most extensive, can be found
in the Farrand, Elliot, and Tansill collections. Works that reproduce
the Anti-Federalist essays are: *The Complete Anti-Federalist*, ed. Herbert
J. Storing with Murray Dry (Chicago, 1981); *The Anti-Federalist: An
Abridgement*, ed. Murray Dry (Chicago, 1985); *The Essential
Antifederalist*, ed. W. B. Allen and Gordon Lloyd (Lanham, MD,

extended republic theory advanced by Madison, even small, homogeneous republics could not long survive the ravages of faction. The doctrine of the separation of powers, as explained in *The Federalist* and embodied in the Constitution, was modified to meet the requirements of a republican government and thereby separated from the concept of "mixed government" with which it had been so closely associated since ancient times. And the division of authority between the state and national governments was without historic parallel, as was the creation

1985); *The Anti-Federalists,* ed. Bruce Frohnen (Washington, DC, 1999); *The Debate on the Constitution: Federalist and Antifederalist Speeches, Articles, and Letters During the Struggle over Ratification,* ed. Bernard Bailyn, 2 vols. (New York, 1993); and *The Antifederalist Papers,* ed. Morton Borden (East Lansing, MI, 1965). Commentaries on *The Federalist* include: David Epstein, *The Political Theory of* The Federalist (Chicago, 1984); Garry Wills, *Explaining America:* The Federalist (1981; repr. New York, 2001); George W. Carey, The Federalist: *Design for a Constitutional Republic* (Urbana, IL, 1989); *Saving the Revolution,* ed. Charles R. Kesler (New York, 1987); and selected Martin Diamond articles in *As Far as Republican Principles Will Admit,* ed. William A. Schambra (Washington, DC, 1992). A scholarly and legalistic account of the Constitutional Convention deliberations is Charles Warren's, *The Making of the Constitution* (Boston, 1928); other highly informative and readable accounts are: Clinton Rossiter, *1787: The Grand Convention* (New York, 1966); Catherine Drinker Bowen, *Miracle at Philadelphia* (Boston, 1966); and Carl Van Doren, *The Great Rehearsal* (New York, 1948).

of an independent and coordinate judiciary with the power of judicial review.

THE AFTERMATH:

TWO COMPETING TRADITIONS

Many conceptual frameworks can be used for the study of American political thought after the founding period, particularly the period from the Civil War to the present, an era toward which scholars in the field take widely divergent approaches. But despite scholarly disputes about the character of the founding period, there is one approach that not only embraces much of the subsequent political thought concerning the nature of the Constitution and its major principles, but provides as well a narrative for understanding the major political controversies that have arisen in the American tradition. To be concrete, the thesis advanced by James Allen Smith that the Constitution betrayed the democratic principles of the Declaration of Independence—a thesis that has gained currency among a large number of American historians and students of American political thought—has also provided the basis for a deeper understanding of major themes in American political thought. But to appreciate why this is so, we must first survey some basic interpretive differences concerning the character of the Declaration of Independence and its role in the tradition.

The meaning of the Declaration and its status within the American tradition have been extensively debated. To begin with, we find significant disagreement about its place in that tradition. On one side are those who emphasize that the Declaration was necessary to secure French assistance for the coming war; that it should be taken for what it professes to be, namely, a declaration severing the existing "political bands" with England and giving the reasons for this severance; that it was in no way an "ordering" document in the same sense as the Constitution, as it provided little guidance relevant to the questions of proper ordering other than the principle of consent; and that, in many ways, it reflects the values and principles of the American tradition up to that point in time and should be understood in that context. To show its continuity with the tradition, the proponents of this view emphasize that the main body of the Declaration lists twenty-eight charges against King George III and that most of them relate either to violations of the common law (e.g., "For imposing Taxes on us without our Consent," "For depriving us in many cases, of the benefits of Trial by Jury") or to disruptions of the processes of deliberative self-government (e.g., "He has dissolved Representative Houses repeatedly," "He has called together legislative bodies at places unusual, uncomfortable, and distant from the depository of the public Records"). On the other side are those who see in the Declaration, to one degree or another, the articulation of goals that are essentially binding commitments. Focusing almost entirely on its second paragraph, which begins "We hold these truths to be self-evident," the proponents of this interpretation look upon the Declaration as specifying the basic values and goals that, in effect, constitute the yardsticks by which to measure the "progress" of the nation, its people, and its political institutions. Those who hold this view often write as if the Declaration marks the very beginning of the American political tradition.

And what of the Declaration's meaning? Generally speaking, the meaning one assigns the Declaration will depend on the status one accords it. Those who fit it into the broader context of the American tradition and take into account the historical circumstances surrounding it are inclined to view it against the background of "one people" declaring independence, with the famous paragraph beginning "We hold these truths" basically reiterating the standard contractual theory the terms of which, as Jefferson intimates, had become part of the political culture. Some point out that Locke's contractual theory meshed nicely with the Protestant covenantal tradition. In any event, viewed from this perspective, the Declaration clears the path for the majority to establish a government most conducive to its well-being. Moreover, in this account, the tradition is seen as continuous, with no serious break between the Declaration and the Constitution.

Those who treat the Declaration in an ahistorical fashion are inclined to read it in a markedly different and more expansive way, typically as an expression of fundamental and eternal truths. Those adopting this position not only embrace the underlying premises of Lincoln's Gettysburg Address but in some ways move beyond them. In claiming that "fourscore and seven years ago our fathers brought forth on this continent a new nation," Lincoln sought to establish July 4, 1776, as the birth date of the nation. Furthermore, in asserting that this "new nation" was "conceived in liberty and dedicated to the proposition that all men are created equal," he lent weight, whether he intended to or not, to the position—promoted by many critics and students of the American system over the decades—that securing equality is among the nation's most basic commitments. He also implied that the degree to which this commitment and others derivable from the Declaration are realized constitutes the supreme measure of the success and worthiness of the institutions created by the Constitution.

Understandably, differences exist over the range and nature of these commitments. America's presumed commitment to equality, for instance, has been understood in different ways. A specific and limited understanding of equality was advanced by the abolitionists who, in the decades immediately preceding the Civil War, used the "all men are created equal clause" to advance their cause. The equality mentioned in the Declaration, in their view, stemmed from the proposition that in the state of nature men are equal, that no man is superior to another. From this flows the belief that legitimate government, one based on the consent of the governed, comes about through a compact between equals. And, since no man is the master of another, it follows that all should enjoy equal rights and treatment by the institutions of government. In these terms, then, slavery is totally at odds with the political morality of the Declaration, and with the passage of the Civil War amendments—the Thirteenth, Fourteenth, and Fifteenth—the constitutional system took a gigantic step toward living up to the basic ideals of the nation.

But a far more expansive understanding of the Declaration's goals is held by many students of the American political tradition. For them, democracy is primarily government "for the people," not necessarily "by the people." Like Croly and Parrington, they hold that the commitments of the Declaration apply to virtually every aspect of society and individuals' ways of life. These commitments, in other words, bear a close relationship to those that inspired the French Revolution. They include, but are by no means limited to, the encouragement of self-sacrifice for the good of the wider community, the discouragement of acquisitiveness in business and the professions, and the promotion of policies that reduce great disparities of wealth, ensure the availability of meaningful work, and guarantee decent wages and living standards. Though the particulars may vary from individual to individual, those who accept Lincoln's understanding of the founding and hold an expansive conception of our national commitments judge the emergence and development of American democracy or republicanism from a teleological perspective, that is, according to the degree to which the political system has lived up to the promises derived from the Declaration. In recent decades, this teleological understanding, no doubt inspired by the Declaration's emphasis on "unalienable Rights," has focused on the protection and advancement of individual and minority rights—economic, political, social—as important measures of the success of the constitutional order.

In this regard, the addition of the Bill of Rights shortly after the ratification of the Constitution is generally perceived by those who embrace this teleological outlook as a conscious effort to advance the democratic "spirit" of the Declaration. It is commonly said or implied that the more important rights in the Bill of Rights not only go a long way toward bringing the Constitution into line with the goals of the Declaration, but also that they are far more important in securing the ends of the Declaration than is the Constitution. While such an interpretation is understandable from the teleological perspective, students familiar with the circumstances surrounding the adoption of the Bill of Rights are inclined to dismiss it. Madison, who can legitimately be regarded as the father of the Bill of Rights, had to walk a fine line in getting the first Congress to agree to what are now the Constitution's first ten amendments. On the one hand, the Federalists opposed the addition of rights for two main, interrelated reasons: first, they thought that adding provisions against abuses that the national government had no power to commit would clearly imply that the Constitution had established a system wherein Congress possessed plenary powers, rather than simply delegated powers; and second, they believed that enumerating certain rights would disparage those not enumerated. Madison, keenly aware of these arguments, sought to dispel any such illusion through what are now the Ninth and Tenth Amendments.

On the other hand, the Anti-Federalists—the principal proponents of additional rights during the ratification struggle—sought above all the specification of "rights" that would weaken the national government (e.g., a requisition process for direct taxation; confining the national government to the exercise of "expressly" delegated powers; greater state control over national elections). The notion of advancing the goals or ideals of the Declaration was far from their intention. But Madison offered up rights that would not, in his words, "endanger the beauty of the Government in any one important feature, even in the eyes of its most sanguine admirers." His efforts were clearly intended to garner greater support for the new Constitution without adding provisions or rights that would in any way weaken the new government.

Taken as a whole, the teleological approach is clearly at odds with that position which views the Declaration as both compatible with the Constitution and as part of the broader American experience that stretches back to the

---

The following works deal with the drafting, organization, underlying theory, and other matters surrounding The Declaration of Independence: Carl Becker, *The Declaration of Independence: A Study in the History of Political Ideas* (1922; repr. New York, 1948); Garry Wills, *Inventing America: Jefferson's Declaration of Independence* (New York, 1978); and Pauline Maier, *American Scripture: Making the Declaration of Independence* (New York, 1998). For works that deal with the "two traditions" question see: Willmoore Kendall and George W. Carey, *The Basic Symbols of the American Political Tradition* (Washington, DC, 1995); Harry Jaffa, *How to Think about the American Revolution* (Durham, NC, 1978); Garry Wills, *Lincoln at Gettysburg: The Words that Remade America* (New York, 1992); M. E. Bradford, *Original Intentions* (Athens, GA, 1993); Gordon Wood, *The Radicalism of the American Revolution* (New York, 1992); and Ross Lence, "Thomas Jefferson and the Declaration of Independence: The Power and Natural Rights of a Free People," *Political Science Reviewer* 6 (1976). Regarding the Bill of Rights see: *Creating the Bill of Rights: The Documentary Record from the First Federal Congress*, ed. Helen Veit, Kenneth Bowling, and Charlene Bickford (Baltimore, 1991); and *The Roots of the Bill of Rights*, ed. Bernard Schwartz, 5 vols. (New York, 1980).

earliest settlements. This latter perspective emphasizes the development of democracy or republicanism in terms of the institutions or processes by which decisions are made rather than their content. Far from seeing egalitarian ends at the center of the founders' understanding of democracy— or, for that matter, as central to the American experience prior to the Revolution—this approach sees popular government, tempered by the need for ordered liberty and the rule of law, as constituting the heart of the American tradition. For this "procedural" school, the Constitution, understood as an "ordering" document that balances these concerns, best embodies the ideals of American democracy.

CONTINUING CONCERNS

The preceding examination of differences over the Declaration's place in our tradition and its meaning provides a useful framework for understanding the main currents within American political thought since the Civil War. From these varying accounts emerge those issues and concerns that stand at the center of contemporary disputes about the nature of American constitutionalism. We can see this most clearly by examining developments regarding the basic distribution of powers and authority prescribed by the Constitution: its "vertical" character, or federalism, the division of authority between the state and national governments; and its "horizontal" character, or the separation of powers, the division of powers and functions between the legislative, executive, and judicial branches of the national government. In this endeavor, the teachings of *The Federalist* prove useful both for gauging the degree and direction of change and for supplying a fuller background for understanding contemporary controversies and positions.

FEDERALISM

Two major issues connected with the principle of federalism have arisen in the course of the American experience: the foundations of union—that is, whether the union is a contract between the states or whether it is based on the assent of the people; and the extent of national powers vis-à-vis those of the states. As the following survey will indicate, these two issues are to some extent interrelated.

FOUNDATIONS ❧ The relationship between and relative powers of the state and national governments were bound to be points of contention once the constitutional system was set in motion. It is commonly believed that the Union victory in the Civil War settled the major issues involved with federalism. To a degree, this is true. Certainly the Civil War settled the question of whether the Constitution is to be regarded as a compact between the states or whether it is an "organic" act of one people. At an early point under the new government, in the Kentucky Resolutions that he drafted in response to the Alien and Sedition Acts (1798), Thomas Jefferson contended that state legislatures possessed the authority to nullify acts of Congress that in their judgment exceeded the constitutional powers delegated to the national government. Later, in his *Discourse on the Constitution and Government of the United States*, John C. Calhoun set forth more fully the theoretical grounds for nullification and spelled out a procedure for its use consistent with the processes used for ratification of the Constitution. Calhoun and Jefferson's position regarded the Constitution as a contract between the states or, as Calhoun would put it with more precision, between the sovereign authority (i.e., the people) of each state. In this account, no agency of the national government, including the Supreme Court, could legitimately resolve disputes between the national

point of view; laws, to be supreme, must be pursuant to the Constitution, which is the very question at hand. Lincoln's position, set forth in his First Inaugural Address (1861), goes outside of the Constitution, so to speak, to rebut the contract theory of union by claiming that the union preceded the Constitution. In this organic conception of union, the meeting of the First Continental Congress in 1774 marked the beginning of a process that continued through the Declaration, the Articles of Confederation, and the Constitution, one of the purposes of which was "to form a more perfect union." Indeed, from this perspective it was the people operating through a national agency, the Second Continental Congress, who created the states by declaring independence from Great Britain. But the net effect of Lincoln's formulation is to shift the focus of debate from the Constitution to the status of the states under the Articles of Confederation.

Calhoun's *Disquisition on Government*—a work that, as we have remarked, is considered by many to be one of the few lasting contributions to Western political theory by an American—can be viewed as an outgrowth of this pre–Civil War controversy over the nature of the union in the face of the impending conflict between the North and

South. Beginning with an organic conception of the origins of society and government not unlike that set forth by Aristotle, Calhoun develops the thesis that the only way to prevent oppression and abuse by either government or popular majorities is to give each interest affected by the decisions of government a veto power that it can use to protect itself. His system, in other words, calls for a "concurrent majority" or concurrent consent, whereby majorities within each of the affected interests would have to approve a policy before it could be implemented. Some commentators have observed that Calhoun's concurrent majority system accurately describes the typical pluralistic political process at the state and national levels today, wherein the opposition of significant interest groups more often than not is sufficient to block potential legislation.

Essentially, Calhoun argues that the Constitution does not provide protection against oppression and abuse of power by majorities. He rejects, in effect, the extended republic theory advanced by Madison, arguing that a multiplicity and diversity of interests only hastens the advent of oppressive government. He places no faith in constitutional restrictions designed to keep the national government within its constitutional boundaries because, he argues, majorities will eventually interpret such provisions in a manner to advance their interests at the expense of minorities. Nor, for essentially the same reason, did he believe that the separation of powers could stay the hand of oppressive majorities. He goes to great lengths to show the need for a concurrent majority system, not only to provide protection against abusive government and popular majorities, but to discover, in ways simple majority-rule systems cannot, the true sense of the community.

As a defender of slavery, Calhoun's motives in writing the *Disquisition* have been called into question. Nevertheless, his work can profitably be read as a critique of the Constitution and its fundamental principles. Moreover, Calhoun's major concerns—e.g., how to prevent tyranny and oppression, how best to determine the refined sense of the people—are perennial. But although Calhoun's arguments on behalf of the concurrent majority-rule system provide ample food for thought, there is no denying the strength of his critics' arguments, which call into question the practicality of his system. These criticisms apply also to the proposed means for resolving state-national conflicts in accordance with the principles dictated by his contract theory of union. In either case, delays would be encountered in resolving conflicts or differences, and adherence to the concurrent majority principle could even lead to deadlock, leaving the government incapable of taking necessary action. Likewise, a minority of states with relatively small populations could thwart national initiatives supported by a majority of states and large popular majorities. Calhoun, of course, downplayed these possibilities, arguing that necessity would be the mother of compromise. Nevertheless, these considerations are one reason why the organic theory of union, the principles of which allow for a more expedient process of resolution, holds sway today.

EXTENT ?❧ Whether or not the outcome of the Civil War, a prudential assessment of the historical record, or considerations of practicality dictate an answer to the controversy surrounding the nature of the union, there still remains the problem of delineating the jurisdictions of the state and national governments. Some have suggested that the framers' answer was procedural and was embedded in the Connecticut Compromise; that is, by providing for equal state representation in the Senate and for the election of Senators by the state legislatures, it was felt that the states would have the means to block any national measures that might intrude upon the sovereignty of the states. There is evidence to believe that many of the delegates at the Constitutional Convention most protective of state prerogatives believed that state interests were adequately secured through these provisions. This constitutes what can be appropriately termed a "political" solution to jurisdictional controversies.

The Federalist and the state ratification debates, however, provide grounds for a different understanding of where the appropriate line between state and national authority should be drawn, namely, that there is a constitutional delineation of authority that Congress cannot violate. In this view, substantial powers were to remain in the sole possession of the states, and the Supreme Court bore the responsibility for upholding this constitutional division of powers, thereby insuring that neither side would encroach upon the legitimate domain of the other. This understanding, because disputes over jurisdiction are to be settled by the Court with reference to the Constitution, can be seen as a "constitutional" solution.

Underlying each of these means for accommodating or resolving state-national disputes was the belief that the states would play a major role in the new political system, that they would still exercise significant powers. But over the decades, particularly in the twentieth century, the role of the states has declined enormously relative to that of the national government, so that today many observers contend that the states are in virtually all matters subordinate to national authority. This decline is generally accounted for by pointing to: (1) the early decisions of John Marshall's Court that upheld national authority at almost every turn; (2) the Civil War and its aftermath, particularly the Fourteenth Amendment, which has been subsequently used by the Supreme Court to monitor state and local legislation and practices; (3) the direct popular election of senators mandated by the Seventeenth Amendment, which removed a procedural protection for the states' residual authority; (4) the passage of the Sixteenth Amendment, which eventually provided the national government with the financial resources to exercise control over the states; and (5) the sweeping judicial interpretation of the Constitution's commerce clause, which has given Congress almost unlimited power over local matters and concerns once regarded as well within the reserved powers of the states.

There are, however, more basic reasons, both theoretical and political, for the decline of the states. For instance, one cannot ignore the emergence of Progressivism, the main goals of which were set forth by Herbert Croly. Aside from calling for far greater regulation and control of large business concerns by government, Croly believed that a more equitable distribution of wealth would help advance the national promise by eliminating class conflict. But above all, he wanted to alter the character of the social and economic environment in which individuals lived and worked. To do this required, in his view, basic changes in human motivation: individual acquisitiveness, fostered by the dominant American tradition, would have to be replaced by disinterestedness and the promotion of "desirable competition." Indeed, individual interests would have to be accommodated to the collective good and the need for social advancement, an accommodation best realized, he thought, by promoting "the principle of human brotherhood."

Croly was fully aware that the realization of his national promise required a strong central government. But he also knew that the then-prevailing understanding of federalism, an understanding embraced by both the Court and, to a great extent, Congress, severely limited the scope of the national government's powers. More specifically, this prevailing understanding of federalism—which had substantial roots in the understanding of state-national relations at the time of the founding—held that the powers of the national government were limited by the reserved powers of the states, a limitation that severely restricted the capacity of the national government to enact programs that would advance progressive ends. Indeed, prior to the New Deal of the 1930s, the Supreme Court had employed various doctrines to more or less consistently hold that the power to regulate interstate commerce that had been delegated to the national government could not be used by Congress to achieve ends that fell within the domain of the state police powers—that is, matters relating to the health, safety, and welfare of its residents. The realization of progressive goals, then, devolved upon the states, which meant that, in practice, their realization would be far from uniform throughout the country.

The Court used this same conception of federalism to strike down programs central to Franklin Roosevelt's New Deal in the early 1930s. But by 1937, and under considerable political pressure to change course, the Court began to alter its position. In 1941 it fully embraced the other understanding of federalism, one that also had roots in the founding era, by holding, in effect, that the "common constituents" through their elected representatives were empowered to determine the extent of the national government's power to regulate interstate commerce. Thus, the Court's adoption of this *political* solution to the problem of the boundary between state and national authority gave Congress a free hand to use its commerce power to assume "police powers," so long as national majorities supported such measures. In the terms of American political theory, the "common constituent" paradigm derived from *The Federalist*—which allowed Congress to determine, with the support of majorities, the extent of national authority—replaced that paradigm in which states possessed inviolable or constitutionally protected powers. To put it otherwise, we now have a "political federalism," one that depends ultimately on the opinions of the common constituents as reflected by the political branches, as opposed to a "constitutional" federalism, which holds that there is a constitutionally mandated and relatively fixed division of power. (In recent years, constitutional federalism has made a limited comeback, but it remains to be seen if its return will be permanent.)

A major reason why federalism—in modern times almost exclusively conceived of in terms of the division of powers between the state and national governments—still engenders heated controversy is that neither constitutional nor political federalism is without major shortcomings. Constitutional federalism is only viable if some test or principle can be articulated precisely enough to be used by Con-

---

Among the significant works in the American political tradition dealing with the aspects of federalism are: John C. Calhoun, *A Discourse on the Constitution and Government of the United States* in *Union and Liberty: The Political Philosophy of John C. Calhoun*, ed. Ross M. Lence (Indianapolis, 1992; this volume also contains Calhoun's *Disquisition on Government*); John Taylor of Caroline, *New Views of the Constitution of the United States* (1823; repr. Washington, DC, 2000); and Orestes A. Brownson, *The American Republic* (1865; repr. Wilmington, DE, 2003). Other works that reflect differing views on original intention and modern developments are: Raoul Berger, *Federalism: The Founders' Design* (Norman, OK, 1987); Felix Morley, *Freedom and Federalism* (Indianapolis, 1981); *Essays on Federalism*, ed. George C. S. Benson (Claremont, CA, 1961); *A Nation of States*, ed. Robert A. Goldwin (Chicago, 1963); *How Federal Is the Constitution?*, ed. Robert A. Goldwin and William A. Schambra (Lanham, MD, 1982); Samuel Beer, *To Make a Nation: The Rediscovery of American Federalism* (Cambridge, MA, 1993); *Derailing the Constitution*, ed. Edward B. McLean (Bryn Mawr, PA, 1995); C. H. Hoebeke, *The Road to Mass Democracy: Original Intent and the Seventeenth Amendment* (New Brunswick, NJ, 1995); and Ralph A. Rossum, *Federalism, the Supreme Court, and the Seventeenth Amendment* (Lanham, MD, 2001).

gress to determine the proper boundary lines between state and national jurisdiction when it is considering legislation, a task that has thus far proved impossible for the Supreme Court. Political federalism, on the other hand, abolishes all boundaries between state and national authority, vesting a virtually unlimited power in Congress to control distinctly local affairs and concerns to whatever extent it wants. Moreover, there is little question that "political federalism"—as reasonable as its use may be in certain circumstances—has produced a centralization of power well beyond that contemplated by the framers, which many believe poses a threat to liberty.

SEPARATION OF POWERS:
THE CHANGING LANDSCAPE

That the framers regarded Congress as the mainspring of the constitutional system seems apparent from the precautions they took to ensure that it would not encroach upon the prerogatives of the other branches. The Constitution itself attests to the view that Congress was regarded as the predominant branch: its organization and powers are set forth in Article I; it possesses virtually all the powers delegated to the national government; it can "discipline" the other branches through its impeachment and removal powers; and, inter alia, it plays a pivotal role in the amendment process. Beyond this, as even a cursory reading of *The Federalist* will reveal, Congress was considered closest to the people, the branch that best represented the opinions, interests, and concerns of the nation. Consequently, it is not entirely accurate to say that the Constitution established three "equal and coordinate" branches. The branches are clearly coordinate, each with different functions, but they were hardly deemed equal to one another in their capacity to control and direct the resources and activities of society.

Nothing has changed constitutionally to diminish the authority or powers of Congress. In fact, if one looks at the amendments to the Constitution, the powers of Congress, on the whole, have increased. However, it is clear that Congress no longer enjoys the predominant position the framers accorded it. Just as the nature of federalism has changed, so too has the prevailing understanding of the separation of powers principle. Furthermore, as with federalism, these changes in outlook seem to correspond closely with the rise of Progressivism, that is, with the belief that the national government ought to take an active role in achieving social goals presumably consonant with the spirit of the Declaration of Independence.

THE RISE OF THE MODERN PRESIDENCY ?❧ There are milestones to be noted in the metamorphosis of the original understanding of the authority and functions of the different branches of the federal government. The emergence of political parties starting with Jefferson served to alter the relationship between the president and Congress, but the roots of a more basic change in the perception of the presidency occurred with the 1828 election of Andrew Jackson. The manner of Jackson's nomination, stemming as it did from outpourings of popular support, not only spelled the end of "King Caucus"—the nomination of presidential candidates by congressional caucuses—but also gave rise to the claim that the president was as true and faithful a representative of the people as Congress. Jackson's assertion to this effect, however, did not by itself permanently alter institutional relationships. Until the time of Lincoln and the Civil War, the constitutional system operated pretty much in accord with the vision projected by *The Federalist*, there being but two instances of judicial review (including the ill-fated *Dred Scott* decision) and some fifty-two presidential vetoes, the most significant ones based on constitutional rather than political grounds.

By the turn of the twentieth century, however, Jackson's claim had gained ground, if only by indirection. Theodore Roosevelt, an early champion of many progressive causes, set forth an expansive "stewardship theory" of presidential power. According to this theory, in striving to meet the needs of the nation the president is not obliged to find authorization in the Constitution; rather, he may undertake necessary measures so long as they are not specifically prohibited by either the Constitution or legislation. Woodrow Wilson, who also shared the progressive vision, as early as 1879 suggested that a cabinet form of government, like that which was then evolving in Great Britain, might simultaneously provide for greater accountability and a more energetic executive. To this end, Wilson set forth the broad outlines of a reform of the American political system that may well have served as the basis for a more detailed reform proposed by leading political scientists at the midpoint of the twentieth century. Later, in his classic, *Congressional Government* (New York, 1884; repr. New York, 1956), Wilson lamented the diffusion of power among committee chairmen in Congress, a diffusion that he believed rendered responsible and accountable government next to impossible. Finally, in his *Constitutional Government in the United States* (New York, 1908; pbk. New York, 1961), published only four years before he was elected president, he foresaw the vast potential of the presidency, emphasizing that it was the only national office and that a president could speak with a single, clear voice, whereas Congress spoke with many. Wilson could readily envision presidents, as head of their parties and with the support of the people, providing a steady leadership that would make the presidency the preeminent branch of government. In this he anticipated many of the modern arguments that tend to support presidential supremacy—for example, the argument that the president embodies the "general will" of the people because he alone can discern the overriding national good, unlike Congress, which represents partial and special interests.

Theodore Roosevelt and Woodrow Wilson, each in his own way, paved the way for the modern presidency. With the election of Franklin Roosevelt in 1932 and the subsequent enactment of New Deal policies, the progressive vision first set forth by Croly became a reality. The concept of constitutional federalism was abandoned, the president's role as chief legislator was solidified, and the public came to accept, even to demand, an energetic and positive government. But with the advent of the New Deal and the expansion of the national government and its activities, a serious problem arose that remains unresolved. Simply put, by using very general terms in describing the purposes of its legislative policies (e.g., a cleaner environment, control over the airwaves, safety in the workplace) Congress has given wide discretion to the president and the bureaucracy in implementing them. Many serious scholars contend, not without reason, that Congress has actually delegated its legislative powers to the executive branch in violation of the constitutional maxim that the legislature may not delegate those powers delegated to it by the people.

Still another concern, which has intensified with the advent of the modern presidency, relates to the president's authority in the field of foreign affairs and his powers as commander in chief, which have been used to lead the nation into war even though the Constitution expressly gives Congress alone the power to declare war. Early congressional debates concerning these powers fully reflect more modern concerns. The controversy surrounding

George Washington's Proclamation of Neutrality in 1793, which declared that the United States would remain neutral in the war between England and France, prompted a "debate" between Hamilton and Madison, writing respectively as "Pacificus" and "Helvidius," over the role of the president in formulating and executing foreign policy. Over the decades, Hamilton's position, which accorded the president wide latitude in foreign policy, has prevailed, with Congress assuming a distinctly secondary role. Likewise, the early debates during John Adams's presidency over the deployment of newly commissioned frigates reveal an acute awareness that the president could deploy them in a way that led to hostilities, leaving Congress with no alternative but to declare war. Nevertheless, on the basis of prudential and practical considerations Congress concluded that the president must have such discretion, though he would be ultimately accountable for its exercise. While history provides many examples of the presidential commitment of armed forces to hostilities without congressional authorization, the issue has become more acute in modern times: Franklin Roosevelt's diplomacy, according to some scholars, was designed to lead the United States into World War II by prompting an attack; Harry Truman committed than the leader of a political party; he also has the best claim—far better than that of Congress—to being the representative of a national majority. These developments—coupled with the emergence of radio and television, which have further eased the path for modern presidents to become the leaders Woodrow Wilson envisioned—provide the basis for the claim, which goes even beyond that made by Andrew Jackson, that modern presidents are "more" representative of the people than is Congress.

To return to the broader framework of American political thought, then, it is not surprising that most of the "strong" presidents, the ones most frequently ranked as the

---

On the presidency and the Constitution, see John Adams, "Thoughts on Government," in Bruce Frohnen, *The American Republic* (Indianapolis, 2002); *Separation of Powers—Does It Still Work?*, ed. Robert A. Goldwin and Art Kaufman (Washington, DC, 1986); Paul Eidelberg, *The Philosophy of the American Constitution* (New York, 1968); James Burnham, *Congress and the American Tradition* (Chicago, 1959); James MacGregor Burns, *The Deadlock of Democracy* (Englewood Cliffs, NJ, 1963); M. J. C. Vile, *Constitutionalism and the Separation of Powers* (rev. ed., Indianapolis, 1998); William B. Gwyn, *The Meaning of the Separation of Powers* (New Orleans, 1965); *Reforming American Government*, ed. Donald L. Robinson (Boulder, CO, 1985): Keith E. Whittington, *Constitutional Construction* (Cambridge, MA, 1999); Theodore Lowi, *The End of Liberalism* (New York, 1979); and Willmoore Kendall, "The Two Majorities" in *Willmoore Kendall Contra Mundum*, ed. Nellie Kendall (New Rochelle, NY, 1971).

"greatest" by historians and political scientists—e.g., Jefferson, Jackson, Lincoln, Roosevelts I and II, Wilson—are those who fit within the progressive tradition, that is, those who presumed to speak and act for the democratic ideals of the founding and the basic aspirations and convictions of the people. In fact, some students of the presidency contend that to secure a national majority a presidential candidate has no choice but to adopt the rhetoric and goals of Progressivism: presidential candidates are practically obliged to speak abstractly or in terms of "high" principle in order to avoid offending large voting blocs and influential interests. The net effect of this reality, some believe, is that the presidency by its very nature will ordinarily be an institution that advances progressive values.

THE MODERN JUDICIARY ❧ Many contemporary students of American politics contend that the Supreme Court now makes those decisions that have the greatest impact on individuals and their ways of life. Whether or not this is true, it is certainly beyond dispute that over the years, and particularly since World War II, the Court has fashioned highly controversial decisions that have had an enormous impact on American politics and society. It is also beyond dispute that the Court has moved well beyond the role marked out for it by Hamilton in *The Federalist*. Thus has the separation of powers principle, already altered by the emergence of a powerful executive, been further transformed.

The Supreme Court has been at the center of controversy since the beginning of the republic. The fundamental question, one that has been thoroughly debated by students of the American system, is whether the framers intended for the Court to possess the power of judicial review, that is, the power to nullify acts of Congress. One strong argument, which suggests that this power was usurped by John Marshall in *Marbury v. Madison* (1803), maintains that if the framers had intended the Court to possess this power, they would have spelled it out in the Constitution, just as they did the presidential veto. Others contend, also persuasively, that judicial review is the logical outgrowth of the theory of constitutionalism that was widely shared at the time of the founding. It is unlikely that this issue will ever be laid to rest.

In any case, judicial review is now part of the American political landscape, so firmly established that it is questioned by few outside the groves of academe. Indeed, certainly throughout most of the twentieth century, the Court as an institution has enjoyed the firm support of the American people. No matter how unpopular its decisions, the prevailing political morality is that they must be accepted and enforced. This much is attested to by the rebuff dealt Franklin Roosevelt, at the height of his political power, when he sought to "pack" the Court with his appointees in order to overcome its rejection of key New Deal measures. But it was not always thus. Jefferson and Jackson, for instance, interpreted the separation of powers doctrine to mean that the president was entitled to exercise his judgment about the meaning of the Constitution in deciding whether to enforce or abide by the Court's decisions. Lincoln held to the view, articulated in the context of the *Dred Scott* decision, that the Court was fully capable of making erroneous decisions, and that while they should be obeyed, efforts should be directed at overturning them as soon as possible. It is clear as well that during the Civil War he placed his duty to preserve the union above all else, including his obligation to obey and execute judicial orders.

Most of the Court's controversial decisions have either directly or indirectly involved basic constitutional principles or provisions and their application within a given social or political context. In fact, the roots of Progressivism can be traced to the latter part of nineteenth century and the early years of the twentieth, when the Court used the Fourteenth Amendment and the principle of substantive due process to limit the exercise of the states' police powers, while it simultaneously protected the interests of large business conglomerates, often by narrowly construing federal powers. A case that illustrates the Court's decision-making in this regard, and the one most frequently cited to illustrate the excesses of the Court of this period, is *Lochner v. New York* (1905), wherein a majority of the Court voted to strike down a New York state law setting limits on the working hours in bakeries. Using substantive due process—that is, looking to the substance of the law and its purposes, rather than to the processes of its enactment—a majority of the justices found this law to be an arbitrary and unreasonable limitation on the individual's liberty of contract, and therefore an unconstitutional exercise of the state's police powers. But since the Constitution provides no protection for "liberty of contract," this decision amounted to little more than the Court substituting its will for that of the legislature concerning the need for such legislation.

The *Lochner* decision is important for understanding the nature of the controversies that have arisen in more recent decades concerning the role of the Court. As some commentators have pointed out, there is a parallel between the Court's *Lochner* decision and *Roe v. Wade* (1973), which struck down state laws prohibiting abortions. In both cases the Court employed substantive due process, the difference being that *Roe* was based on a "right of privacy," a right which, like "liberty of contract," is not to be found in the Constitution. In both cases, moreover, the Court substituted its will for that of the state legislature in weighing individual liberty against the well-being and norms of society. But modern critics of the Court emphasize what they consider to be a significant difference between *Lochner* and the decisions in the 1930s that invalidated New Deal policies on the one hand, and the more controversial post–World War II decisions such as *Roe* on the other. In the earlier cases, the Court in striking down legislation merely reinstated the status quo ante, whereas in certain of its post–World War II decisions—most notably the desegregation cases of the mid-1950s and *Roe*—it not only overturned existing law but ordered the states to institute new policies that it maintained were dictated by the language of the Constitution.

The charge that the modern Court has in fact engaged

in legislating, thereby intruding upon Congress's domain, lies at the heart of contemporary disputes about the Court's proper role. Originalists, those who see the mission of the Court in the same light as Hamilton—that is, as upholding the constitutive will of the people as expressed in the Constitution—argue that the Court has been acting ultra vires, beyond its constitutional authority. Most of the Court's defenders—the activists, sometimes referred to as "non-interpretivists"—do not dispute that the Court has legislated. Some see the Court as making up or correcting for the failures of Congress, as in the 1950s desegregation cases. Others, developing a more general theory of judicial power, see the Court as authorized, whenever the opportunity presents itself, to advance basic values, such as human dignity, that are tacitly embodied in the Constitution or the Declaration of Independence. Still others view the Constitution as a "living" document, with the Court, sensitive to the values derived from the Declaration, providing much-needed updates and modifications in light of changing social values and practices. The teleological understanding of the American political tradition is most starkly revealed in these conceptions of judicial power. For many close students of the American tradition, they raise cussion of the separation of powers, the basic problem associated with expansive theories of judicial power is that they promote the concentration of legislative and judicial powers in one body, the Supreme Court.

Apart from these more theoretical concerns, the specific area of the Court's activity that has aroused the greatest controversy is its interpretations of the "due process" and "equal protection" clauses of the Fourteenth Amendment as applying to the states. As we have seen, in the latter part of the nineteenth century the Court employed the "due process" clause to invalidate state legislation concerning economic regulations, working hours, and the like. More recently, the Court has "nationalized" most provisions of the Bill of Rights by incorporating them into the "liberty" of the "due process" clause that prohibits "any state" from depriving "any person of life, liberty, or property, without due process of law." The Court has used this portion of the Fourteenth Amendment to strike down hundreds of state laws dealing with the rights of the accused, procedure in criminal cases, aid to religious schools, capital punishment, libel and slander, school prayer, obscenity, sodomy and pornography, and abortion. Using the Fourteenth Amendment provision that prohibits the states from denying "to any person within its jurisdiction the equal protection of the laws," the Court has ordered states to bus school age children to distant schools in order to achieve greater racial integration, and it has ordered states to follow the "one man, one vote" rule in apportioning seats for both the state legislatures and the House of Representatives. Combined with Congress's use of the commerce power, which allows it to regulate many concerns once thought to be well within the realm of the states' reserved powers, the Court's application of the Fourteenth Amendment has further reduced the residual sovereign authority of the states, particularly in those areas of greatest concern to localities.

The Fourteenth Amendment illustrates the interplay between American political theory and history. It was ratified under questionable circumstances shortly after the Civil War and by all accounts was intended to uphold the civil rights of the newly freed slaves in the South, not to drastically alter the federal design. That much is clear from the congressional debates surrounding the Fourteenth Amendment. Toward the end of the nineteenth century, however, it was seriously advanced that the Fourteenth Amendment and the "liberty" of its "due process" clause embraced or incorporated the major provisions of the national Bill of Rights (that is, the provisions of the first eight amendments to the Constitution). The Court rejected this interpretation until 1925 (*Gitlow v. New York*), after which, starting in the 1930s, it began to incorporate provisions of the Bill of Rights against the states with increasing frequency. And of course, the Court has also "discovered" rights derivable from those actually mentioned in the Constitution, such as the aforementioned "right to privacy."

Clearly the Court has moved well beyond the role envisioned by Hamilton, reaching, as one observer has put it, a "new plateau" of judicial power that in important particulars contravenes the very basis of the argument set forth by Hamilton in justifying judicial review. The notion, for example, of a "living Constitution" is incompatible with the "fundamental law" argument presented by Hamilton and Marshall, an argument logically derived from the framers' understanding of "constitutionalism." The crucial question that emerges is whether the republican processes and the legislative function of Congress as spelled out in the Constitution—in other words, that which marks out how laws and binding decisions are to be made in accordance with the principle of republicanism—have not been overridden by the Court; whether, to put the matter somewhat differently, the theory that justifies judicial activism really does not call for a regime quite different from that established by the Constitution.

Now a justification of judicial activism can be derived from those accounts of the American political tradition that view the Constitution and the ends of the framers as inimical to the republican or French Romantic impulses of the people. In its modern form, this argument would assert that partial or "special" interests control the political

---

On the judiciary, see Christopher Wolfe, *The Rise of Modern Judicial Review* (New York, 1986) and *How to Read the Constitution: Originalism, Constitutional Interpretation, and Judicial Power* (Lanham, MD, 1996); Charles S. Hyneman, *The Supreme Court on Trial* (New York, 1963); Gary McDowell, *Equity and the Constitution* (Chicago, 1982); Raoul Berger, *Government by Judiciary* (1977; rev. ed., Indianapolis, 1997); William Gangi, *Saving the Constitution from the Courts* (Norman, OK, 1995); Keith E. Whittington, *Constitutional Interpretation* (Lawrence, KS, 1999); John Hart Ely, *Democracy and Distrust: A Theory of Judicial Review* (Cambridge, MA, 1980); Ronald Dworkin, *Taking Rights Seriously* (Cambridge, MA, 1977); Michael Perry, *The Constitution, the Courts, and Human Rights* (New Haven, CT, 1982); Bruce Ackerman, *We the People*, 2 vols. (Cambridge, MA, 1991); *The Reconstruction Amendments' Debates*, ed. Alfred Avins (Richmond, VA, 1967); and James B. Thayer, "The Origin and Scope of the American Doctrine of Constitutional Law," *Harvard Law Review* 7 (1893).

processes, that society is structured to perpetuate the power of wealthy elites, that there are few channels through which "common" citizens can make their weight felt. The distinctly political institutions established by the Constitution, in other words, do not fulfill the promises embodied in the expansive teleological interpretations of the Declaration of Independence. The one institution capable of advancing these goals, so this argument continues, is the Supreme Court. The Court, so conceived, is a leader, a trailblazer, leading the American people to a greater awareness and realization of the values that gave birth to the nation.

REPUBLICANISM, LIMITED GOVERNMENT, AND THE PROBLEM OF VIRTUE

In theory, at least, republics would seem to depend much more than monarchies or aristocracies on the virtue of the citizenry. Madison put this proposition in a slightly different fashion when he wrote that "Republican government presupposes . . . a higher degree" of those "qualities in human nature, which justify a certain portion of esteem and confidence." This understanding was widely shared at the time of founding. Indeed, in the sermons and essays before, during, and after the founding period, recurring questions centered around how a people could retain the virtue necessary for self-government—what practices and beliefs might undermine their virtue, by what means might their baser appetites be restrained—and how civility, a sense of individual responsibility, respect for other individuals, and concern for the permanent interests of the community might be cultivated. Yet, if we look to the deliberations at Philadelphia, the Constitution itself, or even *The Federalist,* we find no acknowledgment or treatment of these and like questions, much less answers as to how to cultivate the virtues necessary for a republic. Nor do we find in *The Federalist* much attention devoted to the matter of how to perpetuate a "constitutional morality" necessary for the effective operation of the constitutional system into the indefinite future. It is as if the framers believed the system would run itself once set in motion, without the need of any underlying morality.

What accounts for this seeming lack of concern? Two answers are commonly advanced. First, there are those who, following the liberal paradigm discussed earlier, see the system as anchored in interest, not virtue. If we look, for instance, to the solutions that Madison offered for controlling the effects of majority factions and maintaining the constitutional separation of powers, we can readily perceive his reliance on the competition between and the "channeling" of interests. The framers, as some would have it, believed that out of the competition between multiple and diverse interests the common good would emerge as a matter of course, just as competition in the economic realm eventually produces better products at a lower cost for consumers. Some modern "pluralists," those who view interest-group conflict as the key to understanding the essential nature of American politics, seem to hold this position by virtue of their rejection of the notion that there is an objective common good above or apart from the competitive struggle between interests.

But many other scholars, while not denying the role of interest competition, still regard virtue as the bedrock of the constitutional order. They contend that interests must be bound by "rules of the game"; that all societies must provide moral and ethical limits to interest-group activities, limits that transcend and thus are not part of the competitive process. Accordingly, societies set bounds on the methods that interests may use to advance their ends, as well as on those ends which citizens, individually or collectively, may legitimately pursue. Moreover, the resolution of conflict between interests is often determined by a sense of equity, proportionality, or fairness derived from and supported by the prevailing social morality. From this perspective, then, virtue is essential for establishing and maintaining the moral parameters of interest-group activity, if only to avoid fractiousness and instability.

Thus, a second answer to why the framers were largely silent on the issue of virtue acknowledges that fact while also arguing that the framers believed that the states, churches, local associations, and other groups would serve to nourish the virtue necessary for an orderly and decent republican regime. This answer seems reasonable in light of the fact that the new national government was a limited one, confined to the exercise of delegated powers, largely those related to functions that the states could not execute individually or effectively.

But the maintenance and cultivation of virtue, however that is achieved, remains an especially significant concern for the constitutional order and its operations. While there are admittedly many dimensions to this concern, a

crucial one—all the more so in light of the political centralization that has taken place since the New Deal era—
relates to the capacity of virtue to operate as a barrier to
oppression, either by popular majorities or government.
The framers were well aware of the dimensions of this problem. As Hamilton took pains to point out in *The Federalist*, for instance, if the national government is entrusted
with the task of defending the country against foreign en-
emies, it must possess virtually unlimited authority. Even
Calhoun, who was anxious to restrain government, ada-
mantly maintained that the defense of the nation requires
"the full command of the power and resources of the community." Indeed, it was this realization that prompted
Calhoun to devise his concurrent veto system. Ultimately,
of course, even his system relies on cultivating an appropriate constitutional morality so that disappointed majorities will abide by the rules. More generally, the problem
comes down to whether sufficient virtue, through one
means or another, can be brought to bear to prevent the
abuse of these vast powers, either by majorities or by the
elected rulers.

At the time of the founding, many shared Washington's
view that religion and education could serve to prevent tyr-

anny and oppression. Others, including Madison, maintained that religious teachings, as well as the "republican" civic virtues, would not be sufficient to curb factious majorities bent on abrogating the rights of others; he believed that the "pull" of immediate self-interest was too strong to be overcome by "moral or religious motives." Still, Madison did think that virtue would infuse the constitutional system through the election of "fit characters," a position that he stressed in his debate with Patrick Henry in the Virginia Ratification Convention and outlined in *Federalist* 10. For Henry, however, dependence on virtuous representatives was a "slender" protection; he wished to guard against the "depravity of human nature" with "proper checks," leaving nothing to chance. Clearly, both positions ultimately depend upon some degree of virtue residing in the people. In Madison's case, for instance, the people must be able to identify "fit characters"—that is, they must know what constitutes "fitness"—and they must be prepared to vote for them. This need for virtue among the people was a point also driven home by Hamilton when he wrote in *Federalist* 84 that the security for "liberty of the press," and presumably other liberties, "must altogether depend on public opinion, and on the general spirit of the people and of the government."

The Madison-Henry debate reveals a difference in emphasis on how best to prevent the abuse of power. Henry's position—in contrast to that of Hamilton or Washington—places an emphasis on institutions, on checks and balances within the government to stay the hand of rulers or factious majorities. And his position seems to have permeated our collective conscience; in public discussion about how to protect individuals and minorities from majority oppression or the abuses of government, emphasis is usually placed on institutions. For example, the Supreme Court has come to be viewed as the chief guardian of the Bill of Rights, since that institution, above all others, is charged with protecting minorities from majority oppression. Indeed, as we have seen, the modern court is heralded by many for advancing individual and group "rights" well beyond those envisioned by the framers.

Yet this reliance on institutions is surrounded with difficulties. To begin with, can the Supreme Court, or any other institution, really perform this function over time? Hamilton and Madison, if we extrapolate from what they wrote in *The Federalist*, seemed to hold out little hope that institutions would be able to withstand the force of persistent popular majorities, save as the people had come to venerate those institutions. From their perspective, then, the success of the Court in this capacity relies on the virtue of the people as reflected in their adherence to a constitutional morality that calls for restraint and forbearance.

But this is not the only or most serious problem with this institutional approach. There remains the crucial question of how we can be sure that the institution entrusted with preventing oppression will not itself abuse the powers of government. As both Madison and Calhoun made clear, the institution empowered to limit majorities or prevent the abuses of government might itself act in an oppressive manner. Short of this, the limiting institution might act in a counterproductive way or in a manner that does not serve the end entrusted to it—a charge that, as we have seen, many have leveled against the Supreme Court, particularly in its activist mode. The Court's interpretation of rights, for example, especially those relating to speech, the press, and religion, have been and continue to be the source of enormous controversy. In the first place, that the Court's interpretations correspond with the intentions of those who drafted or ratified the First Amendment is highly questionable. It is to be noted, for instance, that before and at the time of the founding, the traditional distinction between "liberty" and "license" prevailed.

This distinction, in turn, rested on the conviction that God-given rights contained within them the constraints of the "natural law." That is why it was commonly believed that an individual could enjoy greater or more perfect liberty in civil society than in the state of nature, where there was no common authority to impose the restraints of the natural law. The major problem for legislators in the civil society was to make sure that any constraints they did place on behavior corresponded with the natural law. Consequently, and contrary to many modern formulations, their understanding of liberty did not embrace a licentious, do-your-own-thing philosophy that in many instances serves to undermine public morality.

Critics contend that in recent decades the Court's decisions regarding the liberties of the press, speech, and symbolic expression have contributed to cultural debasement and the coarsening of manners and morals. Furthermore, they maintain that the Court, in supposing since the latter half of the twentieth century that a metaphorical "wall of separation" ought to exist between church and state, has exhibited a hostility towards religion, thereby undermining the very institutions that bear a significant responsibility for nurturing the virtues necessary for republican government. As with its understanding of liberty, the modern Court's understanding of the proper relationship between the state and religion is markedly different from that which prevailed during the founding era. For instance, it is commonly noted that six states at the time of the ratification of the Constitution still had established religions. And the connection between the state and religion persisted long after the founding period. In his *Familiar Exposition of the Constitution*, a text completed in 1840 (repr. Washington, DC, 1986) and designed for students in the common schools and academies of Massachusetts, Justice Joseph Story maintained that it was the "general, if not universal sentiment in America . . . that Christianity ought to receive encouragement from the state" and that "to level all religions, and to make it a state policy to hold all in utter indifference, would have created universal disapprobation, if not universal indignation."

Why modern Courts have adopted a wall-of-separation stance regarding religion and the state is a matter for speculation. Their decisions on this and related issues, however, have been and are of great interest to students of American political thought because they often stem from a developed, if unarticulated, understanding of the American political tradition. That is, the positions that the Court has taken with regard to rights, liberty, and religion are not without foundations. In recent decades, for example, they have placed a premium on toleration and the ideal of an "open society," one that is tolerant of and receptive to different opinions and ways of life. The Court's stance towards religion is, in part, intended to defuse an issue that some still believe could lead to serious social upheaval; that is, by walling off government from religion, the Court can be viewed as keeping a sensitive and highly divisive issue out of the political arena.

Much more could be and has been said about the Supreme Court, its role with regard to limited government, and the problem of virtue. But this should not obscure our major concern, which is whether the modern reliance on courts and rights—either the Bill of Rights or rights derived from the Declaration—to prevent the abuse of power by government and majorities is misplaced. As we have already noted, the more traditional understanding says that it *is* misplaced, that to effectively secure limited government one must ultimately depend on the attitudes and morality of the people, and that without a virtuous people, constitutional provisions or structures aimed at preventing oppression will not suffice, at least not in the long run. Yet there remain questions concerning the traditional under-standing. Many individuals, while deeply concerned about cultivating and sustaining virtue, share a libertarian belief that government is hardly the institution best suited to the task of elevating the moral character of its citizenry—that, in fact, to entrust the government with this function is potentially dangerous. Thus, a matter that will be debated for decades to come is to what degree government ought to help private-sector institutions and associations in this endeavor.

❧

While questions surrounding limited government, virtue, and republicanism are among the most widely debated and discussed in the field of American political theory, there are a host of other significant issues: Are our foundations basically secular or are they rooted in the natural law tradi-tion of the West? Is America committed to the realization of certain goals derived from the Declaration, such as so-cial and economic equality? Or is the nation's basic com-mitment not to equality but to self-government through the forms and processes of the Constitution? Is our Con-stitution malleable, to be interpreted in light of the Declaration as circumstances require? Or is it fundamental law in the sense Hamilton and Marshall defined it, to be changed or altered only through amendment?

These issues, will continue to be discussed in the broader context of competing versions of the American political tradition, versions that differ over whether our republican heritage is teleological or procedural in character, and over whether a highly centralized political system is consistent with the framers' vision. One thing is certain: Centralization—a requisite for the realization of the ideals and goals put forth by the teleological understanding of our political tradition—has changed the character of our

---

For more reading on the matters discussed in this final section, consult Graham Walker, *Moral Foundation of Constitutional Thought: Current Problem, Augustinian Prospects* (Princeton, NJ, 1990); *The Moral Foundations of the American Republic*, ed. Robert Horwitz (Charlottesville, VA, 1986); Charles S. Hyneman, *The American Founding Experience: Political Community and Republican Government* (Urbana, IL, 1994); Edward S. Corwin, *The "Higher Law" Background of the American Constitution* (Ithaca, NY, 1955); Philip Hamburger, *Separation of Church and State* (Cambridge, MA, 2002); Robert A. Nisbet, *Quest for Community* (New York, 1978); Graham Walker, "Virtue and the Constitution: Augustinian Theology and the Frame of American Common Sense" in *Vital Remnants* (Wilmington, DE, 1999); and Philip A. Hamburger, "Natural Rights, Natural Law, and American Constitutions," *Yale Law Review* 102 (1991).

constitutional order, altering not only the relationship between the state and federal governments and the separation of powers principle, but also the traditional boundaries between the realms of state and society.

NOTES
ॐ

¹ *The Federalist* consists of eighty-five essays written by Alexander Hamilton, James Madison, and John Jay and published in various New York papers under the pseudonym "Publius" between October 1787 and May 1788 to help secure ratification of the Constitution in the state of New York. These essays are generally considered to provide the best insight into the theory underlying the forms and processes of the Constitution.

² *Democracy in America* is readily available in different editions. It was originally published in four editions; the first two appearing in 1835, the final two in 1840. This work is generally regarded as the most insightful of all commentaries on American society and culture by a foreign observer. In 1888, James Bryce, an Englishman, authored a two-volume work, *The American Commonwealth*, that is also highly regarded, though its approach differs markedly from Tocqueville's. Bryce produced two later editions of his work, the last published in 1914. Gary McDowell has produced the definitive edition of this work (Indianapolis, 1995).

EMBARKING ON A LIFELONG PURSUIT OF KNOWLEDGE?

Take Advantage of These New Resources & a New Website

The ISI Guides to the Major Disciplines are part of the Intercollegiate Studies Institute's (ISI) **Student Self-Reliance Project,** an integrated, sequential program of educational supplements designed to guide students in making key decisions that will enable them to acquire an appreciation of the accomplishments of Western civilization.

Developed with fifteen months of detailed advice from college professors and students, these resources provide advice in course selection and guidance in actual coursework. The project elements can be used independently by students to navigate the existing university curriculum in a way that deepens their understanding of our Western intellectual heritage. As indicated below, the Project's integrated components will answer key questions at each stage of a student's education.

What are the strengths and weaknesses of the most selective schools?
Choosing the Right College directs prospective college students to the best and worst that top American colleges have to offer.

What is the essence of a liberal arts education?
A Student's Guide to Liberal Learning introduces students to the vital connection between liberal education and political liberty.

What core courses should every student take?
A Student's Guide to the Core Curriculum instructs students in building their own core curricula, utilizing electives available at virtually every university, and discusses how to identify and overcome contemporary political biases in those courses.

**How can students learn from the
best minds in their major fields of study?**
Student Guides to the Major Disciplines introduce students to overlooked and misrepresented classics, facilitating work within their majors. Guides currently available assess the fields of literature, philosophy, U.S. history, economics, political philosophy, classics, psychology, and general history.

Which great modern thinkers are neglected?
The Library of Modern Thinkers will introduce students to great minds who have contributed to the literature of the West but are nevertheless neglected or denigrated in today's classroom. Figures in this series include Robert Nisbet, Eric Voegelin, Wilhelm Röpke, Ludwig von Mises, Michael Oakeshott, Andrew Nelson Lytle, Bertrand de Jouvenal, and others.

Check out **www.collegeguide.org** for more information and to access unparalleled resources for making the most of your college experience.

ISI is a one-stop resource for serious students of all ages. Visit **www.isi.org** or call **1-800-526-7022** to add your name to the 50,000-plus ISI membership list of teachers, students, and professors.